W9-ADP-462

A Singer and Her Songs

A Singer and Her Songs

ALMEDA RIDDLE'S BOOK OF BALLADS

EDITED BY
ROGER D. ABRAHAMS

Music Editor, George Foss

BATON ROUGE
LOUISIANA STATE UNIVERSITY PRESS
1970

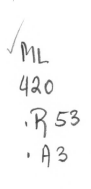

To John Quincy Wolf

DISCOVERER AND FRIEND

This is Granny Riddle's book. She recorded it for me; I transcribed and edited it. There is a lot that needs saying about Granny's life and her songs, but I want her to have the first say, and then I'll have mine.

ROGER D. ABRAHAMS

Acknowledgments

Many have assisted us in the task of putting this book together and it seems appropriate to tip our hats to them. We are first of all indebted to John Quincy Wolf, who discovered Mrs. Riddle's immense store of songs; to Alan Lomax, who first brought Granny to the attention of folksong lovers around the country; and to Ralph Rinzler, who first introduced Granny to us.

Mrs. Bess Lomax Hawes contributed to some of the original conversations that led to the book and her perceptions, as always, brought out important features of Granny's aesthetic. Debbie Galoob Rugh transcribed many of the tapes. Mrs. Frances Lee typed the manuscript in a number of forms. And most important, my wife Mary not only helped out with the interviews and kept the children away at appropriate times but kept us all happy during some very trying hours.

The preparation of the music requires special thanks to Phyllis Dickinson, who cheerfully labored with the first steps of musical transcription, and to Alton Baggett, whose artful manuscript is visible throughout this book.

Contents

I   My Father, His Life and His Singing   3

II   Other Family Singers—Especially Uncle John   26

III   Childhood Days and Courting   50

IV   Brother Russell, Aunt Fanny Barber, and

Other Singing Friends   80

V   Children's Songs and Classics   117

VI   Things That Intrigue Me and Keep Me Busy   124

Afterword   147

Editorial Note and Musical Analysis   161

Appendix I, Notes to the Songs   173

Appendix II, Other Songs in the Repertoire   180

Appendix III, Contents of Ballet Book   190

A Singer and Her Songs

CHAPTER I

My Father, His Life and His Singing

I don't remember when I began singing. About the time I began talking, I suppose, and that goes back awhile, because I was born in 1898. November 21, 1898. And now at seventy-one I still do quite a lot of both singing and talking. Never learned how to stop either, and I guess I won't ever. The first ballet* I remember learning was the "Blind Child's Prayer." I saved it and this was the real beginning of my collecting ballads and songs. This was 1905. In November 25, 1926, we had a cyclone in Heber Springs, Arkansas, in which my husband and baby were killed and as everything we owned was destroyed, so my ballet collection as well as everything else was gone.

After the cyclone, my two little sons and one daughter and I came back to my father's farm in the foothills of the Ozarks. The oldest son, Clinton, nine years, was still on crutches from the crushed leg he got in the cyclone. The youngest, John L., four years old, was still with bandages on his head from a bad scalp wound. The daughter, six years old, was there with my parents, where she had been the four months the boys and I were in the hospital. Here I lived and brought up my children. But I always sang the ballads as did they. We all loved them. I still collected and from memory wrote some down. But until 1949

---

*Pronounced the same as "ballad" by Granny, but she notes that she formerly pronounced it "ballet" as others in her community still do. "Ballet" throughout this volume will refer to a written text; "ballad" to a story-song when sung. (Ed.)

3

or 1950, after the children were married and I had three grand-children, I never had time to really sit down and write all I remembered.

My father was J. L. James. He bought timber, cut timber, worked in the timber for years. And I used to follow him around in the woods. Used to, I'd help saw down a lot of trees when he'd be sawing trees to make a tie or anything. I can carry my end of a crosscut saw. My mother was insistent that I had my lessons—I mean in sewing and everything. She really tried to bring me up a lady. But my father, unfortunately, cooperated with me and brought me up to be a tomboy. He said he had six girls and a boy, and I was the boy.

My father loved his joke. His mother was Irish, full-blooded Irish; her people came here from Ireland. His father was an Englishman. So my father was a mixture. The English are very serious and my father had his serious times, but again he was an Irishman—he loved his joke. If I have any sense of humor, I think I got most of it from my father. My mother was a very fine woman, but you didn't joke around with her as freely as with Dad. She was very serious and ladylike.

My father was a very democratic person. Being democratic, I think, means the equality of all men—that is a *right* to be equal. Now, I think we have to make our own, to more or less make our opportunities, and he did, too. You see, he always told us, "Yes, you've got a right to go just as high as anybody else. But you've got to work your way up." That's the lesson my father taught me. And always to be honest in all things.

I was very close to my father. The very first memory that I have was my father coaxing me to go to bed. I don't know how old I was—I guess about three. And me blackmailing him into, "I will if you'll play me a song on the fiddle, otherwise I won't." And he was coaxing me to go to bed without his rocking me to sleep, which he very often did.

There were four children before me and three children after me. I was the middle child, actually. There were two that died before I was born. I only had one sister older than I and two younger than I that lived, that I ever knew. All girls. I had a brother that would have been next to me, but he died just before I was born. There were four of us girls that lived. Clara was the older, then I. Then Verdie is buried in the Imperial Valley and my sister Irma now lives in Missouri. There's just two of us that's left.

One of the earliest remembrances I have in life was playing with my sister, Claudia, who was four years older than I. We were rocking our dolls to sleep and singing to them. My father, who was a singing teacher, always sang with us awhile almost every night before bedtime. I don't remember the songs we sang while Claudia was with us, but I do remember she sang very well and had a beautiful face, long golden hair, and a very sweet voice. She died after only three days' illness in August before I was six years old. I do remember the day she was taken sick quite well. We sat out in a peach tree in the backyard and sang and ate half-ripe peaches. She said she was getting cold, so we went inside. She was put to bed with a chill, what at that time, 1904, was no unusual thing in Arkansas. There was so much of what people called chills and fever—malaria. And she died the third day of her illness, after two more chills. I had what I guess you would call today a "mental breakdown," and my father had to take me out in the woods with him each day. And for many months I remember I would only cry and say No when I was asked to sing.

Yes, my father bought timber and hammered ties and inspected ties and bought tracts of timber for the Western Tie and Timber Company. He could hew ties, too; but when I was only about fourteen, my father's health took bad and he bought a farm and we moved to the farm and that's when I became a boy. Now, up until then I didn't work actually, I just followed him around for company. But *then* I did, because I plowed and I took care of the horses and broke the colts. I did everything but milkin' cows. I can milk a cow, but I hate to do it. So my younger sister Verdie learned to milk and she did the milkin'.

My father sang every morning when he got up; he sang from a songbook. Every time a new songbook came out, he wanted it. It didn't matter what company put it out, or what song. And he bought this book. But every morning before breakfast, he generally, while mother was fixin' breakfast, I don't ever remember a time that he didn't sit down with his book and sing a song or two. And after supper each night, he'd always sit down and sing awhile. And from the time I can remember, I got 'round and sang, too. I knew my notes before I knew my letters. That is, now, just the first ten lessons, just time and tonality; just how to read a tune. As a matter of fact, that's about all I know yet. I could harmonize a little but not very much.

My father was a vocal teacher, though for years he didn't practice it. He sang all the time. He'd go into any community that we went into, and if they didn't have a singing class, he immediately taught a ten-day school. Those that could pay him, paid him, and those that couldn't, couldn't. And he did a lot more teaching, a lot more work free, a lot more singing . . . as a matter of fact, I don't remember him ever having been paid for any of his teaching or any of this. But he could sing by note. I used to feel he tried to live by note. He was, in many ways, very strict . . . not only with his children but with himself as well.

So he sang most of his songs from the books, but he knew a lot of ballads. This "House Carpenter's Wife" now, I learned that from my father. That is, I learned it and forgot it, and he did too, and then in later years this old man from the hills of Missouri sang it and reminded me . . . I don't know, you see, I think I've always had too much of a love of ballads, and it didn't particularly matter what they were about. Plain bad, good, or indifferent, I just loved ballads. And so to discourage me in this and to get me back to note singing and to help him in the classes, he quit singing ballads for me for a long period of years. I guess ten years that I hadn't heard him sing "The House Carpenter's Wife." Now, he rocked me to sleep with ballads and sang them to me as a little fellow, but when I soon began to know about all the ones that he did, why, he quit singing them to me. And after he died, I found that I had forgotten the words to "The House Carpenter." I could just remember the tune. And this old man was a neighbor of mine that came out of the Ozarks in Missouri, and I heard him sing this same tune and the words.

And I got the words from him, old A. C. Braddy. You know every time anybody will ask a singer where they heard a song, "Well, my great-grandmother . . . ," or "My grandmother . . . ," or "I learned this from my father," or "Somebody . . . and this is just the way she brought it from Holland," until I hardly ever say things about it. But I really think that this version of "The House Carpenter's Wife," I really think that either my great-great-grandfather or grandmother, one, must have brought this across from England.

THE HOUSE CARPENTER'S WIFE

"Well met, well met, my own true love,
Well met, well met," said he,
"I could have been married to a king's daughter fair,
And would have but for love of thee,
And would, but remembered thee."

"Now if you could have married the king's daughter fair,
I'm sure you're much to blame,
For I am well married to a house carpenter,
And I think him a fine young man,
And I proudly wear his name."

"Now if you will leave your house carpenter
And go along with me,
I'll take you where the grass grows green
On the banks of sweet Willie,
And some pleasure we will see."

"Now if I leave my house carpenter
And go along with thee,
What have you to maintain me on
To keep me from poverty,
To keep me from poverty?"

"Well, there's seven ships on the ocean sailing
And the eighth one brought me in;
I've a hundred and ten brave sailor men
Will come at your command,
They'll be under your command."

Then she picked up her sweet little babe
And kisses gave him three,
Saying, "Stay at home with your father, my son,
And keep him company;
And try to remember me."

Then she dressed herself in a scarlet dress,
Oh, she was beautiful to be seen;
And she wrapped herself in a purple robe,
She looked like a gypsy queen;
And she stepped like a gypsy queen.

Now they hadn't been sailing but about two weeks,
I know it hadn't been three,
When this little lady began to weep
And she wept most bitterly,
Oh, she wept most piteously.

And it's, "Why do you weep, my pet?" he said,
"Is it for more gold or store;
Or is it for that house carpenter
We left on England's shore?
You will see him never more."

"Oh, cursed be your gold and silver,
Thrice cursed be your store;
I am weeping for my own little son
I left on England's shore;
Will I see him any more?"

"Cheer up, cheer up, my pet," he said,
"Cheer up, cheer up," said he,
"For as I live you never shall return,
I'll keep you here with me,
And land you'll never see."

Now they sailed on for about three weeks,
I know it was not four,
When the bottom of the ship sprung a leak
And in did the ocean pour;
Then the flames began to roar.

"Oh, cursed be a sailor man,
And cursed the men of the sea.
They've taken me from my house carpenter
And now they are drowning me,
Or else they are burning me."

"What are those hills, my love?" she said,
"They look as white as snow."
"Those are the hills of heaven, my dear,
Where your little baby will go;
But Heaven we will never know."

"What are those other hills, my love,
They look as black as night."
"Those are the hills of Hell, my pet,
Where you and I unite,
Where you and I unite."

I loved my father to sing me that. When I was about seven
years old, I remember him singing it to me. Well, they were
about the same as they are today . . . children and the songs they
wanted. I thought that was a terrible thing, this mother leaving

that baby. That was the thing that struck me the worst, you know, the mother deserting the child. I wasn't too concerned with the husband at that time. I don't know, maybe I subconsciously felt he got what he deserved—he couldn't hold his wife. But the child, I thought that was terrible. For her to ask this child to remember, I still think that it's bad—to ask a child to remember you. And when she drowned, I remembered getting great satisfaction out of the thought that she got her just desserts. Even a child can have thoughts like that.

Now, I really think that this version of "The House Carpenter's Wife" was brought here by the James branch of my family. This man, A. C. Braddy, told me that he had heard this song through the James family, the Missouri branch of the family which was Jesse and Frank's. He lived neighbors to them before he moved to Arkansas. My father's grandfather was a brother of Jesse's father. Robert James was a Baptist minister, Jess and Frank's father was. And a very fine singer Robert James was. As a matter of fact, Jesse James, the outlaw, was a fine singer, so I have been told.

That's right, a fine ballad singer. That I've been told by men that knew him, now. I didn't know him. But my Grandfather Wilkerson fought with him through the War, and he said that he was one of the finest ballad singers he's ever heard. Now Jess was an outlaw, and that wasn't good. But these things happen. My father never mentioned him. He wasn't what you'd call a fanatic in religion, but he was a fanatic in honor. And he believed in leaving these things square. So he never mentioned Frank or Jesse, said he never knew them, glad he didn't. But *his* father did. They were cousins of his father. And he felt that they caused his father so much grief, because they were boys together, and he never mentioned them to me at all. As a matter of fact, a great-uncle of mine told me they were related to us. My father never told me that. I was grown before I knew that they were second cousins. But my father didn't know quite a whole lot about his family, except he had this one uncle on his father's side, but he died when my father was not more than fifteen. His father died when he was real small, four years old, and his mother died when he was nineteen.

So you see, my father knew very little about his folks. There

JESSE JAMES

REPEAT FOR CHORUS

was only his mother and two brothers. We've never been large families. Well, this distant cousin of my father's or a distant uncle or something, he came to our place to spend the night and he told me this: that my great-grandfather and Jesse's father, Robert James, were brothers. He told me the story of the James family. And at that time I was about thirteen. And so the next day I went with my father—I don't know, he was going out in the woods about something and I went with him—and I asked him about this story. And he said, Yes, it was true, he'd always known it. And I said, "Well, why hadn't you . . . "—actually, I felt a little bit proud of the fact that the famous outlaw was a cousin of my grandfather's. And my father made this remark that he was neither ashamed of it, nor proud of it, that he had nothing to do with it. And that I was just to forget about it and not to ask him any more about it, and I never did. If he told you that, you believed what he said. I was never to ask him again, and I never did. But you know, he or my mother sang this version of the song about Jesse, and I never knew that he was part of the family.

Jesse James was a lad that killed many a man.
He robbed the Danville train.
And a dirty little coward that shot Mister Howard
Has laid Jesse James in his grave.
It was Robert Ford, the dirty little coward;
I wonder how he feels,
For he ate old Jesse's bread and slept in Jesse's bed
Then he laid old Jesse in the grave.

    Chorus:
    (Poor) Jesse had a wife to mourn for his life,
    (Three) children that were brave,
    But the dirty little coward (that) shot Mister Howard
    Has laid Jesse James in his grave.

It was with his brother Frank that he robbed the Galatian bank;
He carried the money from the town.
It was at that very place they had a little chase
And they shot old Captain Sheet to the ground.
They went to the crossing not very far from there;
There, they did the same.
With the agent on his knees he delivered up the keys
To the outlaws, Frank and Jesse James.

    Chorus:

It was on a Wednesday night, not a star was in sight,
When they robbed the Glendale train.
And the people they did say, for many miles away,
It was robbed by Frank and Jesse James.
On the next Saturday night, Jesse was at home,
Talking with his family brave.
Robert Ford came along like a thief in the night
And he laid old Jesse in his grave.

Chorus:

The people held their breath when they heard of Jesse's death
And they wondered how he came to die!
It was one of his own gang, called little Robert Ford,
Who shot Jesse James on the sly.
This song was made by Billy S. Slade
Who said when the news did arrive,
There was not a man with the law in his hand
Ever could have took old Jesse James alive.

Chorus:
For Jesse had a wife, she'd lived a lady all her life
And children they were brave
Oh, the dirty little coward that shot Mr. Howard
Laid Jesse James in his grave.

My father was born and reared in White County and Cleburne
County, Arkansas, right up there where they join. It was not in
the Ozarks, but down in the flat counties. And his grandfather
settled this little town called Jamestown in close to Batesville.
And I guess my father was born around Batesville, too, and came
there after his father died. His mother brought him back to her
people, to Cleburne, which is not actually more than twenty-five
or thirty miles. His mother, the Casey's, were Irish, his father
English. Now, his father's brother came back and took care of
them. At that time, you know, there was no what now we call
"relief" and "welfare" for children . . . back right after the Civil
War. And so my grandfather's brother, Hi James, was cowboying
out in Texas, but when my grandfather died, he went back and
stayed there with Grandmother and the children and helped with
the boys until he died.

I guess Uncle Hi must have been a singer too, because my
father learned some songs from him, some cowboy songs he had
learned in Texas. Like this "Texas Rangers" song that I sing.

THE TEXAS RANGERS

Come all you Texas Rangers, wherever you may be,
I'll tell to you a story that happened unto me.
My name is nothing extra, so it I will not tell,
But here's to all good Rangers, I'm sure I wish you well.

It was at the age of twenty I joined the Ranger band.
We marched from San Antonio, down to the Rio Grande.
It was here our captain told us, perhaps he thought it right,
"Before you reach the station, boys, I'm sure you'll have to fight."

And when the bugle sounded, our captain gave command.
"To arms, to arms," he shouted, "and by your horses stand."
I saw the smoke ascending, it seemed to reach the sky,
The first thought then that struck me, "My time had come to die."

I saw the Indians coming, I heard them give the yell,
My feelings at that moment no tongue can ever tell.
I saw the glittering lances, their arrows around me flew,
And all my strength it left me, and all my courage too.

We fought full nine hours before the strife was o'er.
The like of dead and wounded I never saw before.
And when the sun was rising, the Indians they had fled.
We loaded up our rifles and counted up our dead.

All of us were wounded, our noble captain slain,
And the sun was shining sadly across the flooded plain.
Sixteen as brave Rangers as ever roamed the West
Were buried by their comrades, with arrows in their breast.

'Twas then I thought of Mother, who to me in tears did say,
"To you they are all strangers, son, with me you had better stay."
I thought that she was childish, the best she did not know;
My mind was fixed on ranging and I was bound to go.

Perhaps you have a mother, boy, likewise a sister, too,
And maybe you have a sweetheart to weep and mourn for you.
If that be your situation, although you'd like to roam,
I'd advise you from experience, you had better stay at home.

I have seen the fruits of rambling, I know its hardships well.
I have crossed the Rocky Mountains, rode down the streets of hell.
I have been in the great Southwest, where the wild Apaches roam,
And I tell you from experience, you had better stay at home.

And now my song is ended, I guess I've sung enough.
The life of a Texas Ranger, boys, is something very tough,
And here's to all you ladies, I am sure I wish you well.
I am bound to go on roaming, so you ladies, fare you well.

The two James brothers, Robert and Jonas, they came from
Kentucky. I think they didn't stay in Kentucky more than a
generation. My father's grandfather was probably born there
in Kentucky, but I think the great-grandfather came there from
England. I don't think that, actually, they'd been in this country
too many generations when the Civil War came up. Actually, it
must have been after the Revolutionary War that the Jameses
even came here. I don't know where he knew this family history
from. I suppose this old uncle, I guess Uncle Hi had told him
these things. I once asked him something about fighting in the
Revolutionary War, and I just remember he said, "Well, our
folks were in England at that time." He said we weren't even
here. We were English at that time.

Now, I believe in giving the mother all the love and respect
that's due her, but probably I would disagree with you and many
other people. I don't think a mother . . . a mother's love maybe's
a little different to a father's. Her love's tender, but a father's is

strong. I don't think a mother's is any more for a child than a father's. And frankly, if they have to lose either, if they have a good father, I think a child possibly will make out better with a good father than he will a mother. I really do. Though my children lost their father at a very early age. I did the best that I could do alone and I'm proud of it—of the three children I raised—but they'd have had it maybe not as hard just with their father than it was with me. He was equipped to make a better living than I could.

I think maybe I was closer to my father than my mother. I don't think I was a neurotic in it or anything—had a father image in it, or anything like that—but my father and I liked the same things. We liked to sing, we liked to go and to travel. My mother stayed at home and she didn't ever, even to the last day of her life, allow me to travel as much as I liked. As a matter of fact, I doubt she'd be satisfied if she's in Heaven—which I think so—but she could hardly be satisfied if she knew what I was doing down here, traveling all over by myself. But my father would thoroughly approve of it; just go on if I wanted to. Mother used to laugh and say that he had the heart of a tramp and the only reason he stayed at home was because he had the children and had to. And it didn't do a lot. What would take him away was his work, or a singing convention, or some sing. I've known him to walk—people used to walk, of course, more than they do now—but a singing convention, three or four days' singing which they used to have back then—if it was within twenty miles, he went and stayed the whole three or four days. We did like to sing, the both of us, from the earliest. The first song that I ever remember singing with my father was "Old Cottage Home." Now I don't know how old I was, but I was under school age. I'm sure I couldn't have been more than four or five years old. And this song I still love and sing at seventy-one years old.

MY OLD COTTAGE HOME

I am thinking tonight of my old cottage home.
It stands on the brow of the hill,
Where in life's early morning I once loved to roam,
But now it's so quiet, so still.

CHORUS

Chorus:

Oh, my old cottage home
Stands on the brow of the hill,
(Where) in life's early morning I once loved to roam,
But now it's so quiet and still.

Many years have gone by since in prayer there I knelt
With loved ones around that old hearth.
But my mother's sweet prayers in my heart are still felt,
I will treasure them up here on earth.

Chorus:

One by one we have gone from that old cottage home,
And on earth I will see them no more.
But I shall meet them round Heaven's bright throne
Where parting will come never more.

Chorus:

But, of course, usually I couldn't go with him, when he went traveling to these singing conventions or into the woods. But a number of these songs that I still sing today, my father collected in travels, y'see. He'd get those ballets. He'd hear the tune, and he could write this tune out, and then he brought it home. And many of these songs, I don't even know where my father got them. But many of those I use all the time I got from my father. Now this is one of them. I don't even know if this is a folksong or not, but I remember I was very glad of this when he brought it in.

THE BOYS IN BLUE

The office had just opened up
When a man quite old in years,
He entered there and his careworn face
Showed signs of grief and tears.
And when our clerk approached him
In a trembling voice he did say,
"I'm looking for my boy,
He's coming home today."

"I'm afraid you've made a mistake, sir,
But surely you must know
This is an express office
And not a town depot.
But if your boy is coming home,"
The clerk with a smile did say,
"You'll find him with the passengers,
In a depot over the way."

"Oh, you don't understand me, my boy,"
The old man gently said.
"He's coming not as a passenger
But by express instead.
He's coming home to me and mother,"
With tears in his eyes he said,
"He's coming in a long black box;
He's coming to us dead."

Just then a whistle rent the air,
"The express train," someone cried.
The old man rose to trembling limbs
And quickly rushed outside.
And from this train, a long black box
Was lowered to the ground.
The scene was heartbreaking to see
By those who gathered around.

"Be careful, do not handle it rough,
It contains my darling Jack.
He went away a wild, reckless boy,
See how he's coming back.
He's broke his poor old mother's heart,
Her warning has come true.
She said he'd come home to us dead,
When he joined the boys in blue."

This was known at that time through the area, somewhere in the mountains above there where he went. And he collected this on a timber-buying trip someplace from a little girl. Jenny Love. I remember him telling me who wrote it. She wrote this ballet and signed her name to it. Her name was Jenny Love.

He brought home lots of ballets to me. Up until the tornado I had the original copy of every ballet. Now, I only have, unfortunately, a few.

We'd write out ballets on any song that we wanted to remember, and even some that we already knew, if we wanted them in our collection. I guess that my father even did that, for I found a sheet in his hand with a song about the tornado at Heber Springs which I think he and our neighbor, Ruby Dylan, wrote right after the storm. I remember that he sang and hummed around on it, but I never knew he wrote it out until I found it in a box with some of my mother's things in it, pictures and letters and other things. He had the ballet dated—November 25, nineteen-and-twenty-six—in which I was a victim also. "The Storm of Heber Springs" is what he called it.

After my husband and baby were killed, and most of the rest of us were very badly hurt, we had to stay in the hospital. I stayed for four months, and I guess he wrote the song then, while I was in the hospital. That spring he did sing around a little on this. I heard him hum this tune and sing some of these words. I didn't stay around to hear it particularly. I don't think I told him it bothered me, but maybe he thought it did. I know he made it up to some tune of an old song, one that I know but can't place right now.

THE STORM OF HEBER SPRINGS
NOVEMBER 25TH, 1926

'Twas on Thanksgiving Day
The town of Heber Springs
Was visited by a cyclone
And partly swept away.

The people no doubt was feasting
And never thought so soon
That by a dreadful cyclone
They'd shortly meet their doom.

We'd just got home from the Thanksgiving dinner that they'd given at the factory where my husband worked. And we had just returned home when the storm came.

They saw the storm approaching
The clouds looked low and black,
And through that little city,
It left a dreadful track.

They saw the cyclone coming,
And it's too sad to relate
The happiest of families
That had to separate.

They saw lightning flashing;
They heard the thunder roar.
Such tears were in that city
Was never known before.

And as the storm came near them,
They heard the people cry:
"O Lord, have mercy on us!
Is this our time to die?"

Some people in that city
Declared it was God's wrath,
To course the great tornado
To take them in its path.

They pointed to the churches
Where they'd refused to go
To pay to their Redeemer
The debts of love they owed.

I think the churches were all blown down . . . I believe someone told me that the churches were either unroofed or damaged. That's why some people thought that it had been God's wrath. I don't believe things like that part, but then again it's possible.

When the storm came, I was taken to the hospital and stayed there four months. I came back to my parents' home and stayed two or three months. So I was not in the town of Heber Springs. It was rebuilt by the time I went back. Grass was growing over the wreckage. Of course, you could tell where the storm had been. As a matter of fact, I didn't want to visit any of the scenes where it was—and *didn't*. I only went down to where our house was and they had built another house there. And then I turned around and went back. So I didn't do any prying, and I didn't do any asking about this song. I guess I didn't feel like talking about it.

Now, my father, I don't know how to explain him without sounding snobbish. In his songs he was like Child in his collecting, we'll just say like that. If a song had a smattering of suggestive dirt in it, he didn't sing it, and he didn't allow me to.

And so I can't sing many of the plainer ballads now without feeling sort of self-conscious. Perhaps it was prudishness, but then my dad was like that, and he brought me up like that. Now, he wasn't prudish in approach of life. He could discuss anything with you. But in ballads I guess I'm like him.

Now, dirty minds may have made dirty ballads around this "Nightingale" song, but actually that began as a classic. I consider it with "The House Carpenter's Wife," "The Demon Lover," or many of those. Now, my father's version of this is similar to the one of Jimmy Driftwood's father [Neil Morris]. He has it on a record almost like I sing it—almost the tune—not quite, but it's almost. Personally, I've never been able to see anything unclean in the "Nightingale" song, and I've sung it to some pretty big audiences. About three years ago, a newspaper friend of mine—I won't name his name—was the first. In his column he

THE NIGHTINGALE SONG

brought out the fact that Jimmy's father had sung a rather . . .
well, suggestive version, and it was the *same* version that I sing.

One morning, one morning, one morning in May,
I spied a young couple just making their way,
And one was a soldier, a brave one was he,
And the other a lady, oh, a fine one was she.

"Now where are you going?" said the soldier so free.
"I'm going to the river, it's flowing for me;
I'm going to the river and sit by that spring
Just to watch the water gliding and hear a nightingale sing."

"Then may I walk with you, as you journey along?
If I may walk with you, I'll sing you a song.
I'll sing the old concordance that'll make my fiddle ring.
We'll watch the water gliding and hear a nightingale sing."

Said the lady to the soldier, "I'm lonesome and blue,
And I think from your actions that you're lonesome too.
So let's walk together down to that great spring
And watch the water gliding and hear a nightingale sing."

Now they had been there an hour or two
When out from his satchel a violin he drew.
Sang the old concordance and he made his fiddle ring,
Then they watched the water gliding, and they heard
         a nightingale sing.

Said the soldier to the lady, "It's time I should go."
"Oh, no," said the lady, "play me just one tune more.
I'd rather hear you fiddle one tap on those strings
Then see the water gliding and hear a nightingale sing."

So he tuned his old fiddle to a higher key,
Played the "Shamrock of Erin," oh, he played it so free.
He played the "Shamrock of Erin," oh, he made that fiddle ring.
They watched the water gliding and they heard a nightingale sing.

Said the lady to the soldier, "Why don't you marry me?"
"Oh, no," said the soldier, "that never could be.
I've a wife in Ireland and children twice three,
And one wife in the army is a-plenty for me."

"Goodbye," said the soldier, with his parting caress.
"Tomorrow I go back to the throne of Queen Bess.
If I ever come back it will be to this spring.
We'll watch the water gliding and hear a nightingale sing."

"Goodbye," said the lady, she gave him her hand.
"I'll think of you often in Erin's Fair Land.
I'd rather hear you fiddle one tap on those strings
Than see the water gliding and hear a nightingale sing."

Now we can let our dirty imagination run away with us sometimes. I'm glad my father was a clean-thinking man and brought me up to be. 'Cause I just have to see dirt if I believe it's there.

CHAPTER II

Other Family Singers
--Especially Uncle John

Now "The House Carpenter's Wife" I learned from my father, "Black Jack Davey" from my mother. Really from my mother's brother, Uncle John Wilkerson. I've heard my mother sing little snatches of it but she wouldn't have dared sing a song like that. To her it would have been what we call bawdy. As a matter of fact, I just heard her hum along on it and then forbid me to do it, but that's the *sure* way to get me to do anything even yet. Then my uncle wrote it out for me and I sang it. And I've never seen anything particularly bawdy in the song. Those things happened then and they still do today. Shouldn't be, but they do.

There's many versions of this. This one happens to be one my uncle taught me—this "Black Jack Davey." This gypsy Davey came riding by and stole the lord's wife. He did it by his music, his singing and his whistling. Now we had no stories on these as a child; we just felt about like this as we did about "The House Carpenter's Wife" and things like that . . . that she had run off and left her baby, which I thought terribly scandalous and that was my idea as a child, and it still is, as a matter of fact.

BLACK JACK DAVEY

Old Black Jack Davey came a-riding by,
A-whistling so merrily,
He made the woods all around him ring
And he charmed the heart of a lady,
He charmed the heart of a lady.

26

"Come go with me, my pretty little miss,
Oh, go with me, my honey.
I'll swear by the beard upon my chin
That you'll not want for money,
You'll never want for money."

"Pull off, pull off those high-heeled shoes,
They're made of Spanish leather.
Put on, put on the low-heeled boots
And we'll ride off together,
We'll both ride off together."

Now she pulled off her high-heeled shoes,
All made of Spanish leather.
She got behind him on his horse
And they rode off together,
They both rode off together.

That night her husband he came home
Just a-looking for his lady.
Her servant spoke before she thought,
"She's gone with Black Jack Davey,
Rode off with Black Jack Davey."

"Go saddle me up my coal-black stud,
He's speedier than the gray is.
I've rode all day and I'll ride all night
But I'll go find my lady,
And I'll bring back my lady."

He rode all night and at broad daylight
He came to the river a-raging;
And there he spied his darling bride
In the arms of Black Jack Davey,
The arms of Black Jack Davey.

"Pull off, pull off those long blue gloves,
They're made of finest leather;
And give to me your little white hand
And we'll ride home together,
We'll both ride home together."

Oh, she pulled off the long blue gloves,
All made of Spanish leather.
She gave to him her lily-white hand
But said, "Goodbye forever."
She said, "Goodbye forever."

"Would you forsake your house and home?
Would you forsake your babies?
Would you forsake your wedded love
To go with Black Jack Davey?
Go off with Black Jack Davey?"

"I have forsaken house and home,
I have forsook my babies.
I now forsake my wedded love
For I love Black Jack Davey,
I love Old Black Jack Davey."

"Last night I slept on a warm feather bed
Between my husband and babies.
Tonight I sleep on the cold, cold ground
In the arms of Black Jack Davey,
The arms of Black Jack Davey."

Most of them, a majority of my songs, came directly or in-directly through my uncle or my father. But this little song, this "Brisk Young Farmer," I learned that directly from my mother. I never heard my father sing that. She learned it from her mother. I first remember my mother singing this to me in about the year nineteen-and-six. She said she, in turn, learned it from *her* mother, who had known it since she was a child in Tennessee, long before the Civil War.

BRISK YOUNG FARMER

I'll tell you about a brisk young farmer
Who was handsome and renowned;
He courted a fair and lovely maiden
And her name was Mollie Brown.

When his parents came to know this
They were angry and did say,
"We'll send him away across the widest ocean
Where he'll never see her face."

He sailed the ocean over and over,
Then came back to his native side;
Said, "If Mollie is alive and I can find her,
I will make her my lawful bride."

It was early in the morning
And he was walking down the street,
Thinking of his Mollie darling,
When his true love he chanced to meet.

It's "Good morning, good morning, my pretty fair maiden,
Good morning and could you ever fancy me."
"No, my fancy's on a brisk young farmer
Who has gone sailing on the sea."

"Describe him to me, my pretty fair maiden,
Will you describe him unto me?
Perhaps I had a chance to know him,
I have lately crossed the sea."

"Oh, he's proper and very handsome,
He is also slim and tall;
His hair is dark and very curly,
His pretty blue eyes the best of all."

"I guess I saw him and I knew him.
Would his name be William Hall?
I saw a cannon-ball shot through him
And in death I saw him fall."

Such screams, such screams from the pretty fair maiden
Crying, "Alas, what shall I do;
We were parted, both broken hearted:
Now my heart will break in two."

"Cheer up, cheer up, my pretty fair maiden,
Cheer up, cheer up, for I am he.
Now to convince you of my story,
Here's the ring you once gave me."

They joined loving hands together
And to the church did go straight-way;
This young couple were lawfully married
Whether the parents were willing or no.

This Uncle John Wilkerson, my mother's brother, taught me
a lot of the Wilkerson songs that I heard my mother humming

but which she wouldn't teach me. He had a beautiful singing voice, Uncle John, but he liked a lot of songs that my mother didn't like for me to know. He used to sing quite a few silly ones and some that my mother objected to. And those that I was supposed to have forgotten, I didn't, unfortunately. And those that I wanted to remember, I think I've forgotten. He did sing "Froggie Went A-Courting" and this song, "The Dying Soldier."

Now, that one, I still have the ballet to that. I found it, written out in nineteen-and-six, I was eight years old, by my uncle. I have never heard anybody sing it other than myself, and my uncle. And he's been dead many years. I think this must have originated back in Maryland or someplace, because it's about the banks of the Potomac—some kind of war song. Anyway, this soldier was buried there.

THE DYING RANGER

The sun was sinking in the west, and it spread a lingering ray
Through the branches of a lonely forest, where a dying soldier lay.
Far away from his loved New England, 'neath the Southern sultry sky,
On the banks of the Potomac they laid him down to die.

A group had gathered 'round him, they were comrades in the fight,
And a tear rolled down each manly cheek as they bid him his last
        goodnight.
One best friend and loved companion was kneeling by his side,
Trying to staunch the life-blood flowing but, alas, in vain he tried.

Then spoke the dying soldier, "Harry, weep no more for me.
I am crossing death's dark river, beyond it I'll be free.
But listen, Harry, oh, bend closer, and listen to what I say,
I have a story I must tell you, e'er my spirit ebbs away."

"Far away in old New England, in our own dear home state,
There is one who for my coming with a saddened heart now waits.
She's a fair young girl, my sister, my blessing and my pride.
She's been my only joy since childhood, for I've had no one besides."

"We have no mother, she lies sleeping, beneath the graveyard sod.
It's been many long years weeping since her spirit went to God.
We have no father, he was buried years ago in the deep blue sea.
We have no other, we've no kindred, there are just Nell and me."

"Then our country was in danger, the call came for volunteers.
Nell put her arms around my neck, her blue eyes filled up with tears,
Saying, 'Go on my precious brother, drive those traitors from our
        shore.
My heart may need your presence, but your country needs you more.' "

"Now, comrades, I am dying, she'll never see me more.
Day by day she'll wait my coming at our little cabin door.
For I have loved her like a brother, but with a father's care
Have tried in life each grief and sorrow her gentle life to spare."

"And now that I am going, oh, listen to my prayer.
Who will be to her a father and give her a brother's care?"
The soldiers spoke their vow together, like one voice it seemed to fall.
Said, "We'll be to Nell a father, and a brother, one and all."

Up stepped our noble captain, and his tears began to fall.
Said, "Yea, we'll be to her a father and a brother one and all."
Then one sigh of deepest anguish, death's shadow over him spread.
He gave but one convulsive shudder, and the soldier boy lay dead.

On the banks of the old Potomac they laid him down to rest,
With his knapsack for his pillow and a gun across his breast.
Then the soldiers took a vow together, as one voice it seemed to fall.
"Let's be to Nell that brother, and a father, one and all."

Now that one was a favorite of mine. That shows you that a child, you don't know what a child's gonna like. My uncle sang that—he was from Tennessee, Middle Tennessee. They came to Arkansas after he was born—you see, he was the baby of the family—but they went back to Tennessee.

I don't want to think that I was a morbid-minded child, but still I loved these sad songs. Most of my songs, if you'll notice, there's just a cheerful one now and then. I have always felt in sympathy with something . . . well, I think maybe that our best songs are our ballads. You know, happy things that tell us good news don't make the papers as often as sad news. And most of the ballads, didn't you ever notice that, are written about sad occurrences. And my idea on that song is that this must have been a soldier in the Revolutionary War. I believe it must be older than the Civil War, because "drive the traitors from our shore," wouldn't have gotten in there in the Civil War. And I've heard it "drive those Redcoats," too.

I have that song in my Uncle John's handwriting, there at home. I have it in a plastic case, because it's almost falling apart. It's been written close to sixty years ago. It was at home in my mother's family Bible. Most of my song-ballets were destroyed, but this happened to be there. As a matter of fact, I only found it a few years ago in going through her things, and I took out the old family Bible which was my grandmother's. And I found this ballet. And he had dated it the day that he wrote it and had written a little footnote down there, that after so much teasing that he had sung me that song and promised to write the ballet and give it to me if I would go to bed. And that's priceless, that.

I remember the night I stayed with him, even. I went down to spend the night. I think this must have been maybe before he was married. He didn't marry until he was, I think, thirty. And he and my grandfather lived on the old home there alone after we moved away. And well, not alone, because I stayed there a lot of the time, quite a bit more than I stayed at home. And I'd thought that this song that I was telling about . . . well, I had to go, leave. When we'd go off, maybe with my father, from that area, y'know, for a year at a time, sometimes. And then Uncle John would sing that song. I remember the first time I heard that. I was about four or five years old, and we were living out across from there and they took me with them. When we were at home I stayed at Granddad's if I wanted. And I thought that he was thinking about Granddad's home when he sung of his home, his childhood's home.

It was mostly Uncle John that I learned the Wilkerson songs from. He and my only grandfather. You see, my father's father died when he was four years old, and his mother died when he was nineteen, so I never knew them. So my Grandpa Wilkerson, a Confederate soldier in the War Between the States, was the only grandparent I ever knew. His wife, my grandmother, died before I was born. But this thing . . . "Rome County" and "Man of Constant Sorrow" and "Brother Green" are the only songs I ever remember hearing my grandfather sing. He wasn't what you would call a singer.

Well, my grandfather, the story that he told me of "Man of Constant Sorrow"—anyway, this version that I'm doing—this man was a friend of my grandfather's back in their earlier days when he was about eighteen—that was some ten years before the Civil War. And he had some kind of disagreement with his family and the girl that he was getting ready to marry—he had gone there for the wedding and found she'd run off with another man. So, he wrote this song, packed a grip . . . he left and went to California. He sang it before he left and my grandfather had this hand-written copy of it. Maybe this man that gave this to my grandfather had heard an older ballad on "Constant Sorrow" and had just written his song from that. That's what I think. My grandfather at the time was about eighteen and he was about eighteen when the Gold Rush was on. And my grandfather, I think, married, probably not long after that. This boy was about his age and was going to get married and then the girl jilted him and he and his father had this falling out, well, he went to California. It was during the Gold Rush, about '49 or '50. It was in the '50's

MAN OF CONSTANT SORROW

CHORUS

I suppose, but it was several years before the Civil War, which
you know began about '60. I suppose he went to the gold fields,
but my grandfather told me he never heard from him again. So
he didn't know if he made it to California or not, but he kept as,
a matter of fact, this old handwritten sheet.

> I am a man of constant sorrow,
> And many troubles I've gone through,
> But the thing that bows my heart in sorrow
> I will shortly tell to you.
>
> I have some friends who have proved faithful,
> But one to me's been most unkind.
> I'll bow my head like an humble Christian
> And leave my troubles all behind.
>
> [This verse is sung as a chorus.]
>
> I will bow my head like an humble Christian,
> To California I'll go on.
> When I am traveling through the mountains
> I'll cast a wishful look behind.
>
> Yes, when I'm traveling o'er the Rockies
> I'll cast a longing look behind.
> I will pray for the friends who have been faithful
> And forgive the one who's been unkind.
>
> So, fare you well my loving comrade,
> The days I spent with you have been good.
> I'll think of you often by the campfires
> While I am traveling my lonely road.
>
> When I am traveling down the mountain
> I'll think of you whom I've left behind,
> For though some friends have proved unfaithful,
> To me you ever have been kind.

This "Rome County" I also learned from my grandfather. He
claimed to have known the man that wrote this. But since then,
so many people have had so many versions . . . but this is the version I learned from him. Anyhow, this man shot his brother-in-
law and he was condemned to give a lifetime sentence. I remember my grandfather, who was born and reared, married, and lived
in Middle Tennessee until my mother was six (she was the fourth

child), telling me the story of this song and teaching me at least part of these verses. He did say the story was true and did happen in Rome County, Tennessee, back there near where he had lived. I would think it happened just before or right after the War Between the States. I had forgotten some of these verses and Joan O'Bryant wrote out a ballet on it for me. I wrote out for her all I remembered and she finished it for me. When we compared versions we sang it just alike except that she knew all the verses and I had forgotten some of them. Now the last, I believe she did that a little different.

ROME COUNTY

In the beautiful hills way out in Rome County
That's where in my happy boyhood I played.
And that's where my heart keeps turning, oh ever,
But it's where the first mistake in my life I made.

At thirty years old I courted and married,
And Amandya Gilbraith became my sweet wife.
For some unknown reason her brother Tom shot me,
And three months later I took Tom's life.

For twenty long years this wide world I rambled;
I went to old England, to France and to Spain,
But I grew heartsick for the hills of Rome County,
Boarded a tramp steamer and came home again.

I was captured and tried in the village of Kingston;
Not a man in the county would say a kind word.
The jury came in with a verdict next morning;
"A life-time in prison," was the words that I heard.

The train it pulled out, poor Mother stood weeping,
Poor Sister she sat all alone with a sigh.
The last words I heard was, "Willie, God bless you";
Was "Willie, God bless you, God bless you, goodbye."

In the burning hot sands of the foundry I'm working;
Yes, working and toiling my life all away.
They'll measure my grave by the Cumberland River,
Whenever I've finished the rest of my days.

And no matter what happened to me in Rome County,
No matter how long my sentence may be,
I still love my home way back in Rome County,
Way back in Rome County in East Tennessee.

My Grandfather Wilkerson was not really a singer, but for some reason I do remember him teaching me these, I guess because they had stories that stayed with me. And another was this "Brother Green." Granddad did it to the tune of "Barbara Allen"—they did that, you know, using the same tune for different songs.

BROTHER GREEN

Come, Brother Green and stay with me,
For I am shot and bleeding.
I here no more will see my wife
And my dear children.

The southern foe has laid me low,
On this cold ground to suffer.
Stay, Brother, stay, and lay me away
And write my wife a letter.

Tell my dear wife; she prayed for me,
That if while bullets rattle,
That I would be prepared to die,
If I should die in battle.

Tell Father too; he prayed for me,
He prayed for my salvation,
But I have beat him home at last,
Farewell to all temptation.

And that had more verses as he sang it, but I can't call them to mind.

My grandfather gave me the impression—maybe it was just a childish one—that he knew something about this story personally, too. He was a southern soldier. The story that he understood was that they *were* two brothers, two bloodbrothers, brothers in the flesh. One fought for the North, the other for the South. And my grandfather told me he had known that to happen. And then after the battle the southern soldiers were going through the wounded and caring for them. That battle, they had won it. And he found this Union soldier; he went to him. And when he turned him to where he was recognizable, it was his own brother. "Green" was a given name at that time—I knew Green Brewer here, in fact. And it was supposed to be the Brother Green that wrote the ballad. And my friend Martha Willhite heard a very similar story from her mother who taught her the song—so I guess it's true, though she didn't say it was the soldier's brother—just that it was two Civil War soldiers. But that's the story told me by my grandfather who was a Rebel soldier and who died an unregenerated Rebel. I can remember a real scolding from him because I was singing "Yankee Doodle" one time—he didn't allow that. He used to sing "Dixie" . . . taught *that* to me.

Oh, yes, my mother sang ballads. She just loved them. Oh, she liked music, but my father didn't approve of me singing by ear, you know. He wanted me to sing it as it was in the book. He didn't approve of me not keeping up with my music lessons like that. Just digging around and hunting up an old ballad and then spending my whole time singing it. But if a note sounded sweet to me, it didn't matter if it was in the book or not. Which I'm afraid is true yet. My mother sang ballads, and my father knew quite a few, but in early age he quit singing them to me because I guess he thought he was corrupting my chances of becoming a good singer.

Well, here's a little one my mother sang to me as a child. I remember it very well . . . I can remember yet what I'd think when she'd sing this. I'd think maybe this was a girl that had married and gone away from her mother and she was a-crying to go back. I always had a fierce imagination—'fraid I still do have—and she was trying to go back to see her mother and probably it wasn't pleasing her husband. So at night, when she'd sing this, I could picture it that way.

TEN THOUSAND MILES AWAY

On the banks of a lonely river, ten thousand miles away,
I had a dear old mother whose hair had turned to gray.
Oh, blame me not for weeping, oh, blame me not I pray,
For I want to see my mother, ten thousand miles away.

I wish I were a little bird, I'd fly so far away,
To the bands of the lonely river, ten thousand miles away.
Last night, I lay a-sleeping, I dreamed a pleasant dream.
I thought I saw my mother, close by the lonely stream.
Oh, blame me not for weeping, and blame me not I pray,
For I want to see my mother, ten thousand miles away.

Today I got a letter, it's from my sister dear.
She spoke of my dear old mother, and I wish that she were near.
They tell that she's now sleeping in a lonely new-made grave.
My poor old aged mother whose hair had turned to gray.

As years roll on before me, I'll sometimes kneel and pray.
For the banks of the lonely river, ten thousand miles away.
So blame me not for weeping, and blame me not I pray.
I miss my aged mother, ten thousand miles away.

I'm glad to say that I never had to miss my mother much, because I wasn't separated from her much. We lived quite near to
my mother. And my husband only lived nine years and then I
went back to the old farm there to finish bringing up the children

and she lived in a house right close. When my father died in 1933, we moved in together and stayed together nearly as long as she lived. I was fifty-nine years old before I lost my mother, and with the exception of nine years of that time, I had lived either in the house or adjoining house with my mother.

Some of her songs go 'way back. Now, her mother's mother died when she was only seven or eight years old, but she learned this song "Chick A La Le-O" from her mother and taught it to my mother. And my mother taught that to me, and she had learned that from her mother and her mother said she could remember her own mother singing it to her. And I am now singing it to *my* great-grandsons. And as her own mother came from Ireland, she supposed she learned it in Ireland. The Irish grandmother might have just made them up and sung them, as I have many songs that I've just written and sung to my children— that I don't count as folksongs—and it could be that this just began that way.

LA LA LA CHICK A LA LE-O

Chorus:
Oh La La La Chick A La Le-O
Ta La La La Chick A La Le-O
Ta La La La Chick A La Le-O
Tra La La Chick A La Le-O

I'm going to marry just who I please
La La La Chick A La Le-O
I know I will if he'll marry me
La La La Chick A La Le-O

Chorus:

I think I'll marry little Johnny Green
La La La Chick A La Le-O
He's the prettiest boy I've ever seen
La La La Chick A La Le-O

Chorus:

Right now he's off to the wars away
La La La Chick A La Le-O
But he'll come back some pretty fair day
La La La Chick A La Le-O

Chorus:

He'll come a-sailing across the sea
La La La Chick A La Le-O
And he'll come home to marry me
La La La Chick A La Le-O

Chorus:

He is small, just about so high
La La La Chick A La Le-O
But I love him better than chicken pie
La La La Chick A La Le-O

Chorus:

And yonder he comes I do believe
La La La Chick A La Le-O
Oh, Lord, I hope he marries me
La La La Chick A La Le-O

Chorus:

I guess I got a lot of my children's songs from the Wilkersons, from my mother or Uncle John. Like this "Froggie Went A-Courting," that's a Wilkerson family song. Nobody except my family [that] did that just this way. And even then, I have this

FROGGIE WENT A-COURTING

cousin, Jack James, he fights me now on the version of that. He sings that with this "Captain Caro diddy-I" outfit, like that. Jack sings it like that. And he says Uncle Marion Wilkerson taught it to him—that was an uncle that I had and Jack had, my mother's and his mother's brother. Well, Uncles Bill and John taught it to *me* as I sing it—they were Uncle Marion's brothers. And so I finally got this cousin Fanny and asked her, and she said Yes, I was definitely singing the Wilkerson version to it. Which was the side that was Irish, you know. She has the family tree. She claims that it was brought here from Ireland by the great-grandparents—that it's just a family song that we've had traditionally in our family. And I have never heard a version quite like it. But that nothing has been added to that, and we don't dare take one verse from it. Jack sings it just the same, except for the chorus.

Mr. Frog went a-courting and he sure did ride,
To me rop, strop, by, Mr. Gamble.
Had a sword and a pistol buckled at his side,
Singing rop, strop, by, Mr. Gamble.

    Chorus:
    Oh, heemo, himo, keemo, kimo
    Raldy, raldy, ray.
    And a rop, strop, pennywinkle, flanneldoodle, yellow bug,
    A-rop, strop, by, Mr. Gamble.

He rode right straight to Miss Mouse's door,
To me rop, strop, by, Mr. Gamble.
And he kicked so loud that he made it roar,
Singing rop, strop, by, Mr. Gamble.
Then he took Miss Mousy on his knee.
He said, "Please, Miss Mouse, marry me."
Rop, strop, by, Mr. Gamble.

    Chorus:

She said, "Well, I can't answer that."
Rop, strop, by, Mr. Gamble.
"Until you ask my Uncle Rat."
Rop, strop, by, Mr. Gamble.

    Chorus:

Uncle Rat gave free consent,
Rop, strop, by, Mr. Gamble.
Oh, a weasel wrote the publishment,
Rop, strop, by, Mr. Gamble.

Chorus:

Now Uncle Rat he went to town,
To me rop, strop, by, Mr. Gamble.
To buy Miss Mouse her wedding gown,
Singing rop, strop, by, Mr. Gamble.
Where will the wedding supper be?
Oh, way down yonder in a hollow tree.
Rop, strop, by, Mr. Gamble.

Chorus:

And who will the waiters be?
Rop, strop, by, Mr. Gamble.
Well, a pink-eyed gnat and a black-eyed flea,
Rop, strop, by, Mr. Gamble.
What will the wedding supper be?
Well, buttercups and dew-drop tea.
Rop, strop, by, Mr. Gamble.

Chorus:

The first came in was a big white moth.
Singing rop, strop, by, Mr. Gamble.
She spread her wings, made a table cloth.
Rop, strop, by, Mr. Gamble.

Chorus:

And the next came in was Mr. Gnat,
Rop, strop, by, Mr. Gamble.
And he sat down on poor Uncle Rat.
Rop, strop, by, Mr. Gamble.

Chorus:

The next came in was a spotted tick.
Rop, strop, by, Mr. Gamble.
He et so much then he got sick.
Rop, strop, by, Mr. Gamble.
Then the frog came swimming across the lake,
He got swallowed by a big black snake,
Rop, strop, by, Mr. Gamble.

Chorus:

There's a little bit of cornbread on the shelf,
Singing rop, strop, by, Mr. Gamble.
And if you want anymore just sing it yourself.
Rop, strop, by, Mr. Gamble.

Now, there are lots of other animal songs that children from five to forty seem to like. Like this little crowing rooster song. And "Aunt Nancy." And all the children, my children, and all the children I've ever sang it to, my "China Doll" they love that. But then, down at U.C.L.A. at the folk festival they asked for it so much until I became thoroughly disgusted with singing it, as children more than forty years old asked for it most of the time.

CHINA DOLL

Mama buy me a chiney-doll.
Mama buy me a chiney-doll.
Mama buy me a chiney-doll.
Do mama do.

What'll it take to buy it with?
What'll it take to buy it with?
What'll it take to buy it with?
Do mama do.

We'll take Daddy's featherbed.
We'll take Daddy's featherbed.
We'll take Daddy's featherbed.
Do mama do.

Where would our daddy sleep?
Where would our daddy sleep?
Where would our daddy sleep?
Do mama do.

He could sleep in the puppy's bed.
He could sleep in the puppy's bed.
He could sleep in the puppy's bed.
Do mama do.

Where will the puppy sleep?
Where will the puppy sleep?
Where will the puppy sleep?
Do mama do.

Sleep in the piggy's bed.
Sleep in the piggy's bed.
Sleep in the piggy's bed.
Do mama do.

Where will the piggy sleep?
Where will the piggy sleep?
Where will the piggy sleep?
Do mama do.

Sleep in the horse's bed.
Sleep in the horse's bed.
Sleep in the horse's bed.
Do mama do.

Where will the horse sleep?
Where will the horse sleep?
Where will the horse sleep?
Do mama do.

Graze out on our front lawn.
Graze out on our front lawn.
Graze out on our front lawn.
Do mama do.

Where will my children play?
Where will my children play?
Where will my children play?
Do mama do.

They can swing on the garden gate.
They can swing on the garden gate.
They can swing on the garden gate.
Do mama do.

Yes and get a spankin' too.
Yes and get a spankin' too.
Yes and get a spankin' too.
Do mama do.

CHAPTER III

Childhood Days and Courting

Now, when I was a child we lived in lower Cleburne County about thirty miles from where I live now . . . as a matter of fact, where I live now was the Cherokee Strip. And these Indians were in roving bands going by where I lived then. It hasn't been so many years, you see, since those Indians were dispossessed and sent into the Indian territory which joins Arkansas. And this roving band of Indians came back there every summer. And there was a little girl of about my age. And I really liked her, and I went down and visited in the Indian camps often. At the beginning, someone had to go with me, but it was not more than a half mile from where I lived at that time. They'd stay for two or three weeks each summer. And my mother and all of the other women hated to see those Indians come campin' in there. They said they stole everything they could get their hands on. I didn't know if they did or not, and didn't care. At the time I enjoyed them. Anyway, the land was theirs first. If they got a chicken now and then, what did that matter? They didn't have to steal from us anyhow, 'cause my mother, if they ever came and asked for anything, just gave them whatever they wanted. Just food was all they asked.

And so this little girl was about my age. And, I don't know if it was significant in the world of her culture, but she did a little chant. Unfortunately, I've forgotten a lot of it.

NISHI

Nishi had a mater in Chicocka-needle-o
Nishi had a mater in Chicocka-needle-o
Nishi mater kay
Nishi may gay
Gay ta meet her mater in Chicocka-needle-o.

Now, maybe this was not Indian. My mother knew this song, used to sing it. She learned it from someone in her childhood. I don't know if it was an Indian. It seems to me she said it was a German woman. I think there must have been a confusion of many languages, because you can tell there is a little German there, with "Mater."* I guess there's no real language to it because a lot of educated people have tried to identify it. The little

*This is how Granny pronounced the word. (Ed.)

Indian girl, her story of this was that this was a little Indian girl, and her mother went away with the Great White Spirit. That he led her out and went over into another land where there was better hunting . . . the happy hunting ground, you know. So, this little girl would tell me stories about her people . . . and I told her our stories. I may have even taught that song to her, because my mother knew it, but anyhow, we used to sing it together. Being friends just sprang up between she and I. I've sung that song to the kids. It just has a kind of a jolly sound. Now, Mother could translate it:

> Nishi had a mother in the promised land
> Nishi had a mother in the promised land
> Nishi's mother called
> Nishi had to go
> She went to meet her mother in the promised land.

It went on through her father.

Well, the first complete ballad that I remember—now, I was singing before then, but I didn't know the whole song all the way through—was this "Blind Child's Prayer." Someone had written in to this paper, I don't know if it was a newspaper, magazine, or what and asked for the words to the "Blind Child's Prayer." There are these columns, you know, where people write in and ask for old songs. And this was printed. And my mother read it out to me and I thought it was beautiful and she read it to me again. At the time I was barely six years old, but I remember it so well—the deceit I practiced! We were living in an apartment with another man and his children—the mother was dead—Jim Chandler. He had some little kids about my age and so she'd read it to me—two or three times and I'd learned it. I could learn poetry rather quickly, as I can now if it's something that I *want* to retain, and most of the time I don't have a lot of trouble. So, Mr. Chandler came over and I was singin' and she had sung me this tune, and she had sung the piece to me several times and probably read it a couple of times and had sung it maybe for a day or two. I know the next time Mr. Chandler came I told him I could sing the song and he wanted me to sing it, and I said, well, I'd have to go and get this paper so I could

Almeda Riddle.

J. L. and Martha Francis ("Mattie") James, Granny's father and
mother. The girls are her sisters: Clara, eleven; Almeda, six; and
Verda, three.

H. P. and Almeda Riddle, October, 1917.

Granny Riddle singing with Beth Lomax Hawes and the New Lost City Ramblers.

read it. As a matter of fact, I hadn't been to school. I couldn't read at all. And so I got this ballet that she'd clipped out for me—that's the first I remember of my collection, this "Blind Child's Prayer," and I made a big show of singing it off that paper. He just acted like he thought I was really doing it and got up and went on, and after he left then, my mother told me that he knew better. And I felt so cheap I had made such a fool of myself, pretending that I knew more than I did. I think that was the best lesson I've ever had from that day 'til now. I had lot rather that I didn't get too much praise because I always feel just like if I wanted to perform a little or put on or make out like I knew just a little more than what I did—I can still feel that same feeling of shame and humility that I felt. I was miserable for days. Here's the song, but I can't do it as well as I did—at six years old. I don't have the voice I had then, but at least I still know the words and I still remember the lesson.

BLIND CHILD'S PRAYER

They say, dear Father, that tonight
You wed another bride;
That you will clasp her in your arms
Where my dear mother died:

That she will lay her stately head
Upon your manly breast
Where she who now lays low in death
In her last hours did rest.

They say her name is Mary, too,
The name my mother bore;
But, Father, is she kind and true
Like the one you loved before?

And are her steps so soft and light,
Her voice so sweet and mild;
And, Father, do you think she will love
Your blind and helpless child?

Please, Father, do not bid me come
And greet your lovely bride;
I could not greet her here in the room
Where my dear mother died.

Her pictures hanging on the wall,
Her books all lying near.
And there's the harp her fingers touched,
There is her vacant chair.

The chair by which I used to kneel
To say my evening prayer.
O Father, indeed, it will break my heart;
I could not meet her here.

But when I've cried myself to sleep,
And now I often do,
Then softly to my chamber creep,
My new-made mother and you.

Just bid her gently press a kiss
Upon my aching brow
Just as my own dear mother would.
O Father, you are weeping now.

Now let me kneel down by your side
And to our Savior pray
That God's right hand may lead you both
Through life's long weary way.

The prayer was offered and a song was sung
"I'm weary now," she said.
Her father took her in his arms
And laid her on the bed.

And as he turned to leave the room
One joyful cry was given;
He turned and caught her last sweet smile:
His blind child was in Heaven.

They buried her by her mother's side
And raised a marble fair.
And on it were those simple words
"There'll be no blind ones there."

You know every period of time, every century, has some certain thing that it harps on quite a bit. Now, through that period of time when I learned this song, my very closest girl friend had a stepmother. I've known many stepmothers that were a blessing and that the children loved, but my mother always had a sorta' of, I don't know, well, her mother had had a stepmother. Her grandmother was a stepmother and possibly that's it. Anyway, I had this feeling that a stepmother was the very worst thing that could happen to a child. I don't know that I'd been worried so much about losing my mother. But I think maybe that was why it appealed to me. I've always had a very lively imagination and I could imagine how terrible it would be to be blind. And then to be blind and to be helpless and to have a stepmother too; I thought that that was just too much. I think that's maybe why it appealed to me then and I learned it. And I still love that song.

Now don't get me wrong, I think I liked to play games just as much as any other child, but I think that maybe I wasn't so good at them, or possibly that I was more interested in singing than anything else. I remember one day, for instance, when I was about ten years old in 1908 that my older sister and I had gone to spend the day at Mr. Jim Smith's house at Siden, Arkansas, not too far from where we lived. He had two daughters, fifteen and ten years of age. Now the older girls were singing ballads. It was on a Sunday and several girls and boys were there. I sat and listened all afternoon in the next room, and I wouldn't go out and play, which disgusted my ten-year-old friend. Also my sixteen-year-old sister when she found out. She was mad at me for a week, as a matter of fact. Amongst the ten-year-olds and the eight-year-olds that I was playing with, they didn't sing these songs—the older loved song-ballads like "The Lover's Plea," and this other group *would* be sitting around singing. So I got a ballad now and then that way. I can understand Sister's point of view not wanting a ten-year-old hanging around her neck . . . and I think I possibly made a pest of myself. I think I have been a nuisance at many times and many places about my collecting. But there was one song, "Little Lonie," they sang that afternoon which I learned and I remember it still. It was sung twice, once by Miss Smith and again by her boyfriend.

LITTLE LONIE

"I promised I'd meet you out at Adams' Spring
And bring you some money and other fine things."

"Now I brought you no money, let me tell the case;
Leona, let's get married, and there'll be no disgrace."

"Come get up behind me and away we will ride
When we come to yon city then I'll make you my bride."

She climbed up behind him, away they did go,
But they came to deep waters where islands overflow.

"Little Lonie, Little Lonie, going to tell you my mind,
For my mind is for to drown you and leave you behind."

"Jim Lewis, Jim Lewis, won't you spare me my life,
Let me go a-begging if I can't be your wife."

"Little Lonie, Little Lonie, let me explain the case,
As long as you're living, for me it's disgrace."

"No pity or mercy, no pity have I;
Into these dark waters your body must lie."

Then he drowned Little Lonie and he rode away;
And the wide ocean he sailed forth for many a day.

Sailed over the ocean to the other side;
When he thought of Little Lonie and the way she had died.

Then he wrote his confessions, sent them all around
To the friends of Little Lonie that she might be found.

Saying, "Shoot me or hang me, for I am the man
And I drowned Little Lonie in the waters so grand."

Another thing, we would sing walking to school and coming home. I can remember that I first heard "Kitty Wells" this way, and I must have learned a lot of others like that. I remember that I thought it was the most beautiful song. We were going to school and Ella West, who was four or five years older than me, had gotten the ballet of this song. She showed it to me when we met our trails, and she sang it. I went about a half mile and then her road came into mine, so we walked part of the way together. And she said, "I have a new song-ballet," and she was singing "Kitty Wells." I asked her for a written ballet from her and she gave me one. She is one of the few of my childhood friends who still lives in Cleburne County. She is now Mrs. Tom Ghent and lives in Heber Springs.

KITTY WELLS

You ask what makes this darkie weep,
Why I like others am not gay,
And why do tears pour down my cheeks
From early dawn till close of day?
My story, darkies, you shall hear,
For in my heart a memory dwells
For the girl I loved, sweet Kitty Wells.

CHORUS

Chorus:
Oh, the birds were singing, it was morning,
The myrtle and the ivy were in bloom.
The sun over the hill top just dawning,
Then we laid her in the tomb.

I never shall forget the day
That we together roamed the hills;
I kissed the cheek and named the day
That I should wed sweet Kitty Wells.
But death came to my cabin door
And took from me my joy and pride;
And when I found she was no more
I laid my banjo down and cried.

Chorus:

How oft I wish that I were dead
And laid beside her in the tomb.
The sorrow that bows down my head
Is silence of the midnight gloom.
The springtime hath no charm for me
Though flowers are blooming in the dell,
For the bright form that I want to see
Is that of my sweet Kitty Wells.

Chorus:

Now this began as a Negro folksong. The earliest version is like this . . . "What makes this *darkie* weep." I found this back in an old collection just this way, though I've had arguments about its beginnings. And this is the way I heard it as a child.

When I was a kid, just like I am now I was a miser with my songs. When I heard one I liked, I just had to have it. Not everybody kept ballets, though just about everybody sang them. Maybe they'd write out a song until they learned it and then it was thrown down. As a matter of fact, I don't know anybody in my group that did collect them other than myself. But I did.

My group, my school friends, would get together and play and sing right there at the school, just like any kids. We sang this one song "Bonny James Campbell," for instance. We only knew this one verse, back when I was six or eight years old. I think it was Emerson Pickens that sang this one verse and taught us. We called it "The War Song."

WAR SONG

Saddled and bridled and ready for the fray,
He rode away one bright summer day.
Home came his saddle all bloody to see.
Home came his horse, but home never came he.

I didn't even know this was anything until I read about this
in that [MacEdward] Leach's *Ballad Book*, and then I knew it
was part of this "Bonny James Campbell."

Me and my little group used to get out and have camp-meetings.
We sang. I led the singing and did the preaching. And Belle
Ghent always went 'round and talked to the mourners. And
'Medy Pickens, I believe, did the shouting for us. She'd always
come through and get happy and get the Holy Ghost and shout
all over the schoolground. Just children's play.

You see back then we had no radios and we had no TV's, and about the only amusement was that we'd have these games or these sings at the schoolhouse. They are called "entertainments" now, but we called them "exhibitions." Don't know why the word "exhibitions." We'd have memorized poems, you know; I memorized and did some poems, but mostly I sang. I did some recitations. I remember the first one I did. I was five years old at the time. I hadn't started to school yet.

> I went upstairs to ring my little bell.
> Stumped my toe and down I fell.

And I did. I was an exhibitionist even at that age, and I *did* stump my toe and fell completely off the stage and skinned my knee, which was very embarrassing. I think I must have gotten the recitation from the teacher, Arthur Henderson, that was teaching at this country school.

I did this one, "Little Jim," like that. But I did very few recitations, because I was like this mate who was out at sea. He went to the captain and kept stammering and trying to tell him something. So finally the captain said, "Well if you can't tell it, just sing it." And so he sang:

> Should old acquaintance be forgot,
> And never brought to mind.
> The blooming cook fell overboard,
> Now he's forty leagues behind.

Well, like that, I can sing it much quicker than I can say it, so I've always sung my recitations.

When I was about ten years old we left the farm where we were living at that time, while my father was out working in the timber. Mother and we girls were staying at home for a few months. He put in a little store in general merchandise at Edgemont, which was at this time a little stop on this little M. and N. A. Railroad, and they didn't yet have a depot. But we moved up to there and my mother ran this store, while my father bought ties and hammered ties—inspected all up and down the railroad. And they were putting this cut through the mountain.

We lived in the back of the store. I guess there were several thousand people there, living in tents and things—workers, diggers, everything. I don't know where they were from—they just called them diggers—probably Greeks and Italians. I, being my father's delight and my mother's despair, I knew those dirt-train engineers and brakemen. Anyway, I visited amongst them when they came to the store. There was one I especially remember, Little John, that I really liked. He told me many of the customs of the country where he came from—I don't remember where that was, but I think Greece. He was a dark-skinned fellow. It wasn't encouraged, going out and being friendly with them, but I did. Can't watch a kid every minute, not me anyway.

And so one afternoon I was out on the porch watching. They were tunneling the dirt out of this cut. The train had to have an engine behind and one on front to pull over this mountain because it was heavily loaded. And I was standing out there watching the dirt trains go by—they had these boxes in which they hauled the dirt—and this brakeman slipped and fell. I knew the boy. He fell under this train and it took off both legs. I saw the fall, but I didn't go down to see the terrible sight. I saw them take him out and carry him out, and I saw the legs—they were completely off—and I, of course, ran screaming in. My sister and some more girls went down to the track and looked at him until they had to get a train and take him into Little Rock to the hospital (which was the closest at that time), but he died before he got there.

Well, I had heard this song "The Broke-Down Brakeman." I learned it there and then, and "The Broke-Down Brakeman" became for a few years one of those songs which had brought back of lot of memories for me. I learned it then and sang it and remembered this boy. I guess he wasn't so very much older than I was. I was ten—he not more than twenty.

THE BROKE-DOWN BRAKEMAN

'Twas a very cold night in December,
And the winds were driving the snow.
The mercury, if I remember,
Was rapidly falling below.

A warm-hearted young brakeman was retiring,
Retiring from his labors at last.
Three nights and three days without sleeping,
He'd faithfully stood to his task.

He laid his head on his pillow,
And went at once to his dreams;
He dreamed of an oak, of a willow,
And bushes that grew by the stream.

Then he dreamed of his mother and childhood,
Of a schoolhouse that stood on the hill,
Of the bushes that grew in the wildwood,
And of a spring that ran down the hill.

And then he dreamed of his sweetheart,
As she stood there by his side.
'Twas then she'd promised him sincerely,
She'd become his companion and bride.

But the call-boy came at that moment,
Called loudly and rapped on the door.
"Come out of there, Jim, come quickly,
Old pal, your sleeping is o'er."

"Come out of it, Jim, you're a beauty,
Don't let your big red eyes be seen.
Your supposed to be down at 1:30
For the southbound Number Nineteen."

He didn't murmur a moment,
But arose and went to his train.
Like Isaac he marched to the altar,
'Twas not his way to complain.

It was early that very same morning,
They were going on the S. and St. Joe,
They rapidly pulled out of Conway
To meet the next station below.

The cars was a-swaying and rocking,
Jim slipped in between them and fell;
And the rest is so terribly shocking
That the story I'll not try to tell.

But when the last signal was given
And they brought Jim's body from below,
He said, "I hope I'll have a straight run into Heaven,
But not on the S. and St. Joe."

Now, I don't even know what that song is called—I've always just called it "The Broke-Down Brakeman"—but I learned that from another of the brakemen on the little M. and N. A.

My husband and I, I think I was about fifteen and he around sixteen when we began to go steady. And we called it that and we really went steady. I just had no other interest and he didn't, but, of course, marriage was out. Well . . . as a matter of fact, I didn't even think about it. I doubt if he did, at the time. We just liked to be together. We just liked to compare songs and to sing songs. And we were married when he was nineteen and I eighteen . . .

You've heard this "Wexford Girl," "The Oxford Girl," and that? Well, I learned that as "The Oxford Girl." My husband, back when we were sixteen, I don't know where he got it, but he wrote it out for me and sang it as "The Oxford Girl."

It's unusual. I bet these things will intrigue you. I've always had such an inquiring mind. I want to know the beginning of things and once I find it out, then I've lost interest a lot of the time. Now I'd heard my uncle—this uncle that I keep speaking of, Uncle John Wilkerson who came from Tennessee—I had heard him sing snatches of "The Oxford Girl," but I didn't know it completely and in the meantime I was away from him, and my husband knew the song and sang it to me.

THE OXFORD GIRL

'Twas in the town of Oxford
Where I did live and dwell.
In the town of Oxford
I ran a flour mill.

I fell in love with an Oxford girl
With dark and darling eyes;
I asked her would she marry me,
And me she nothing denied.

I called at her sister's house
At eight o'clock one night.
I asked her would she walk with me,
The moon was shining bright.

We'd walk along, I said to her,
In the moonlight's beautiful play.
And if she'd only walk with me,
I'd name our wedding day.

We walked along, we talked along,
Till we came to rough ground.
Then I picked up a hedgewood stick
And knocked that fair maid down.

She fell upon her bended knees;
"Oh, mercy," she did cry.
"Willie, dear, don't murder me here,
I'm not prepared to die."

I paid no attention to her piteous appeal;
I beat her more and more,
Till all around where the body lay
Was in a bloody gore.

I picked her up by her little white hand
And swung her 'round and 'round.
I took her down to the riverside
And threw her in to drown.

Then I went back to my mother's home
'Bout ten o'clock that night.
My mother was very worried;
She woke up in a fright.

Saying, "Oh, God, my son, now what have you done?
You've bloodied your hands and clothes."
The answer that I gave to her
Was bleeding at the nose.

I asked her for a handkerchief
To bind my aching head,
And also for a candlestick
To light myself to bed.

I lay upon my bed,
But still I found no rest,
For the flames of Hell seemed 'round me
And burning in my breast.

I tossed, tumbled all night long
And still no rest could find.
For the flames of Hell seemed 'round me
And in my eyes did shine.

In about a week or so then,
That Oxford Girl was found
A-floating down the river
That led to Oxford town.

Her sister swore my life away
Without a thought of doubt.
Her sister swore I was the only man
Who had led her sister out.

Oh, God, they're going to hang me.
This death I hate to die.
Dear God, they're going to hang me
Between the earth and sky.

And I'd not mind the dying
If I could but find rest.
From this burning, burning, burning Hell,
That's burning in my breast.

When we were courting, my husband visited on Sunday afternoons. In those days we walked mostly. Maybe two or three miles to a singing . . . sacred songs from hymnbooks mostly. We had class at The Crossroads. I was leader of class there for about a year. Every two or three months we elected a new leader, but I did it once for about a year. My father, being a singing teacher, was leader there a lot of the time.

Sometimes, though, when we were courting, we'd just walk along and talk. Most of the times we'd sit on the back porch and talk of books we'd read or things we'd seen or of songs we knew. Sometimes we'd just sing. That was during summertime. In the wintertime, of course, we'd sit there in the house, just as young people sit today. And we'd sing songs to each other just like the kids do now. That hasn't changed much over the years. Young people still sit together singing. They sing different songs, maybe along with the radio or TV, but they still sing. I grant you, the songs don't last as long now as they did then. These ballads we sang, a lot of them lasted from generation to generation. Now, a few months and there's a new one out.

And we used to go to play-parties. One thing we played—
"Pleased or Displeased." One goes around and asks everyone
else, "Are you pleased or displeased?" And if they said they were
displeased, then you said, "What will it take to please you?"
Well, then they told for somebody to have to do something that
pleased them. Maybe he'd have to sing some ballad. Maybe some
boy would have to walk some girl out around the house. That
was very popular. That gave him a chance to walk his girl around
the house. I don't know what kind of kick we got out of it, but
we did. Sometimes it would be half a dozen couples out walking
around. Take a walk down to a certain place and back. And
if we could find some boy that some girl actively disliked, or if
we could get some boy who was really popular and some old
girl that we knew he didn't like—well, it would take that to
please us—he'd either have to sing her a song or walk her out.
Young people just like they are now.

Really, I think we had more fun before radios and TV's. We
did have the old Edison talking machines, that you cranked up . . .
a few people did have. But I think we had more fun when we
just had our organs and guitars and fiddles and play-parties. We
could make our own entertainment then. We'd be just as happy
as can be, sitting around laughing and singing, or playing some
game, or riddling.

There were some that just loved to riddle and could do it for
hours. For the life of me, I can't remember most of them, and
I've tried. They did this one riddle:

> Love I sit, love I stand,
> Love I hold in my right hand;
> I see love, love can't see me.
> If you can undo that you can hang me.

I've heard it unriddled too. This man who was supposed to
be hung had this little dog and his name was "Love." And he
held a part of the dog, he sat upon the dog, and he put some
in the tree to where he could see it.

And another was, "What goes round all over the woods all
day, comes home at night and sits on the table?" That's milk

from a cow. And then we'd have one, "Four fingers, one thumb; has neither flesh nor bone," which would be hard to guess. It was a glove. We'd sit by the fire, spin these tales, maybe tell ghost stories, from when we were little kids on . . . even play these sweetheart games. When I was six I remember I always chose Johnny Ghent and he always chose me. We were sweethearts until we were about eight years old.

I feel sorry for the young people today, running and hunting, running and hunting. Because with war and everything in the nations, and the condition we're in, the kids don't have the security that we had. We could more or less decide what we wanted to do and do it. They can't now. A boy can look forward to doing two or three years in the service.

There are some songs which my husband and I sang together that I don't sing anymore hardly. "The Oxford Girl," for one, which I mess up if I try. And this "Custer's Last Fierce Charge," I scarcely ever do that. He wrote this out for me and I lost the ballet at the time. I can sing it . . . I know all the words, but I never sing it much, though I love it, for it reminds me of singing with him. I learned it from him before we were married, and that was about 1916.

CUSTER'S LAST FIERCE CHARGE

'Twas just before Custer's last fierce charge,
Two soldiers drew in rein,
With a parting word and a touch of the hand—
They might never meet again.
One had blue eyes and curly hair,
Was nineteen just a month ago;
With red on his cheeks and down on his chin;
He was only a boy you know.

The other was a man, tall, dark and stern,
His faith in this world was dim,
He only trusted now in her
Who was all this world to him.
They marched together for many a day,
And rode for many a mile,
But always had met their foe till now,
With a calm and hopeful smile.

But now they looked in each other's eyes
With a look of ghostly gloom,
The tall, dark man was the first to speak,
Said, "Charlie, my hour has come.
We'll ride up yon hill together,
But you'll ride back alone.
Oh, promise me, Charlie, some trouble take
For me when I am gone."

"Upon my breast, you'll find a face,
I'll wear it through the fight;
With dark blue eyes and curly hair,
Like think it is morning light,
It's morning light, it's goodness to me,
In this hour of darkness and gloom,
But little cared I, for the frown of fate,
When she promised to be my own."

"Write to her, Charlie, when I am dead,
Send back this fair, fond face,
Tell her gently how I died
And where is my resting place."
Just then the blue eyes of the boy were dim,
His voice grew husky with pain,
"I'll do your bidding, comrade dear,
If I ride back again."

"But if you ride back and leave me there,
You'll do the same for me.
I've a poor old mother who waits at home,
I'll write to her tenderly.
Among the ones she has loved and lost,
She has buried a husband and son,
And I was the last to my country's call
But she cheered and sent me on."

"Like a weeping saint she stays at home,
Her fond face wet with tears;
It will break her heart, that her last son is gone
When the sad news she hears."
Just then the order came to charge.
The instant hand touched hand.
They answered it and on they rode
This brave, devoted band.

And on they rode to the top of the hill,
Where the enemy with shot and shell
And rifle fire poured into their ranks
And jarred them as they fell.
And yet they reached those mighty heights so hard to gain,
And then the few that Death had spared
Rode slowly back again.

But among the ones who death had claimed
Was the boy with curly hair.
And the tall, stern man that rode by his side
In death lay by him there.
No one to tell the blue-eyed girl
The last words her lover said,
Nor the poor old mother, like a weeping saint,
When she hears that her boy is dead.

May no more sorrow come to her,
God soothe and soften her pain,
Until she crosses the river of death,
And stands by their side again.

We sang a lot after we were married, after supper usually.
We sang as long as we stayed together. He was a good singer as
his father was a good singer. I guess he learned a lot of his songs
from his father, R. W. Riddle. This song that I recorded, the
"Soldier of the Legion," that his father taught to me, he thought
it was a German folksong, but later I found it was published by
Lady Maxwell in 1800 and something. I had always called it a
folksong and learned it as such. Father Riddle learned it from
his mother—she sang it. And my father-in-law was already a
little boy in the Civil War.

A SOLDIER OF THE LEGION

A soldier of the Legion lay dying in Algiers.
There was want of woman's weeping and a dearth of woman's tears.
His comrades gathered 'round him as his life blood ebbed away
And bent with pitying glances to hear what he would say.

The dying soldier faltered as he took a comrade's hand
And said, "I never more will see my own fatherland,
Take a message and some tokens to distant friends of mine;
For I was born at Bengin, fair Bengin on the Rhine."*

*Granny's ballet has "Bengin" for "Bingen." (Ed.)

"When Father died and left we boys to divide his earthly hoard,
I let them take whatever they would and I kept Father's sword;
And with boyish pride I used to hang it where the bright light
used to shine
In our front parlor room at home, our home beside the Rhine."

"Take this sword back to my mother tell her to hang it there
Until there comes another who can it in honor wear,
And please tell my brothers when they meet and gather 'round
To hear my mournful story in the pleasant vineyard ground."

We fought the enemy full five hours and when that fight was done,
Full many a gallant soldier lay dying in the sun
And some of them were soldiers brave grown old in many wars,
The death wound on their manly chests the last of many scars.

But some were young and suddenly they saw life's sun decline
And one of those was their brother who was born beside the Rhine.
"Oh, tell my sister not to weep or mourn with drooping head
When the soldiers come marching home again with glad and gallant
tread."

"But look upon them proudly with calm and steadfast eye,
For her brother was a soldier, too, and not afraid to die.
And if a comrade seek her love, I ask her in my name
To look upon him kindly with no regret or shame."

"Her father was a soldier brave, her brother gives his life
And he has willed his sister dear to be a soldier's wife.
"Tell my sweetheart not to grieve but take another's hand
For I shall never more return to my own fatherland."

"Tell her the last night of my life for ere God's sun be risen
My body will be out of pain, my soul be out of prison.
I dreamed I walked alone with her beside the river Rhine,
Her little hand lay trustingly, confidingly in mine."
Then he looked upon his comrades with calm and steadfast eye,
"Dear comrades, I am going fast; hear you my last goodbye."

I made up a song after my husband's death, to sing to my little boy Lloyd, the baby that was left . . . because he favored him. He was four years old at the time and I sang this to him. Then my granddaughter, Clinton's oldest child Brenda, was born; well, she was the living picture of her granddad so I finished it out and sang it to her. I've sung it to many people, but she claims this is her song. She still loves it . . . I still have to sing her that.

LONG LOST LOVE

My sweet little one, with your winsome ways
And that mop of tangled-curly hair.
You look at me with a look so wise
While you sit and play in your corner there.

Chorus:
Dearer to me, none ever can be.
And nearer, there'll never be none.
For in your sparkling eyes I see
That favor that tells of a long-lost love.

He sleeps out there 'neath the snow tonight,
My long-lost love of yesteryears;
I sit alone by my firelight
And watch your play through scalding tears.

Chorus:

CHORUS

Oh, laugh little one while laugh you may,
For sorrow's gonna come to your heart and I know
Better perhaps for him to be lain
Out there through the drifting robes of snow.

Chorus:

Sweet little one, will you ever know
How much in life you mean to me?
How much of joy and yet of woe
As the favor of him in your eyes I see?

My son Clinton and my daughter Milbry used to pick the guitar and sing a lot. They'd play just about every night after supper, and some of the songs we'd sing along together. Quite a few of the western and cowboy songs I guess I learned from singing with them. They probably got a lot of the songs from an old 78 record or something like that, you know. The kids did that. They had that kind of machine, and he probably heard songs on one of his friend's machine and learned them that way. I don't remember us having one, but some of the other kids did.

This great-uncle of mine, Hi James, was a cowboy that came back there, and I know he sang a good many cowboy songs, like that "Texas Rangers." But he died when I was quite small. And we did have the cattle drive that used to go through the Indian Nation, and I guess we learned some of their songs then. We liked them; they appealed to us. But most of the cowboy songs that I still sing I think came from Clinton or Milbry, one.

But one that I learned from my mother . . . now you're going to recognize this . . . this began away back in England as a young man that died of a social disease. That's right, it did. And then they brought it here and it began as "The Streets of Laredo," but this version is "Tom Sherman's Barroom." Now I love that song, and it was one that Clinton and the rest of us would sing.

TOM SHERMAN'S BARROOM

As I passed by Tom Sherman's barroom,
Tom Sherman's barroom so early one morn,
I spied a young cowboy all dressed in buckskins.
He was dressed in his buckskins nor fit for the grave.

Chorus:
"Oh, beat your drum lowly and play your fife slowly.
Keep up a dead march as you bear me along.
Take me out to the prairie and fire a volley o'er me,
I'm just a young cowboy and I know I've done wrong."

"Oh, once in the saddle I used to go dashing,
Oh, once o'er the prairie I used to ride gay;
But I took to drinking and to card playing
Got shot by a gambler and I'm dying today."

Chorus:

"Will you please write a letter to my gray-headed mother
And state the sad news to my sister so dear;
And there is another that's dearer than a mother
Who bitterly would weep if she knew I was here."

Chorus:

"Oh, bury beside me my knife and six-shooter,
With my spurs on my heel and rifle by my side;
And on my coffin put a bottle of brandy,
Let the cowboys may drink while they ride merrily."

Chorus:

"Will you please bring me a cup of cold water?
A cup of cold water," the dying boy said.
I brought him some water, the words he did mutter,
A gasp and a sputter and the cowboy was dead.

I might have taught that to them, but they could have learned it from a record. Most of the cowboy songs I didn't know as a child . . . I learned them from my kids when they were teenagers . . . songs like "When the Work's All Done This Fall," and "Little Joe, The Wrangler," and "Utah Carrol's Last Ride." I learned them in the 1930's from Clinton, Milbry, Lloyd, or their friends.

WHEN THE WORK'S ALL DONE THIS FALL

A group of jolly cowboys discussing plans one day—
Said one, "I'll tell you something, boys, before I go away.
I'm just an old cowpuncher and here I'm dressed in rags;
I used to be a tough one and on great big jags."

"But I have got a home, boys, a good one, you all know,
Although I haven't seen it since a long time ago.
I'm going back to Dixie once more to see them all;
I'm going to see my mother when the work's all done this fall."

"After the round-up's over, and after the shipping's done,
I'm going back to Dixie before my money's gone.
I have changed my ways, boys, no more will I fall;
I am going home, boys, when the work's all done this fall."

"When I left home, boys, my mother for me cried.
She begged me not to leave her, for me she would have died.
My mother's heart is breaking, breaking for me, that's all,
And with God's help I'll see her when the work's all done this fall."

That very night this cowboy went out to stand his guard.
The night was cloudy and storming very hard.
The cattle they got frightened and rushed in wild stampede;
The cowboy tried to check them, riding at full speed.

While riding in the darkness so loudly did he shout,
Trying his best to check them and turn the herd about.
His saddle horse did stumble and on him did fall;
He'll not get to see his mother, boys, when the work's all done
        this fall.

His body was so mangled, the boys all thought him dead.
They picked him up so gently and laid him on a bed.
He opened wide his blue eyes and, looking all around,
He motioned for his comrades to sit near him on the ground.

"Boys, send my mother my wages, for I'm,
For I'm afraid, dear comrades, my last steer I have turned.
I'm going to a new range, I hear my Master call;
Now I'll not get to see my mother when the work's all done this fall."

"Bill, you may have my saddle, and George, you won my bed,
And, Jack, you take my pistols after I am dead.
But think of me kindly when you look upon them all,
For I'll not see my mother when the work's all done this fall."

Poor Charlie was buried at sunrise, no tombstone at his head,
Nothing but a little board and this is what it said,
"Charlie died at daybreak, he died from a fall;
The boy won't see his mother when the work's all done this fall."

CHAPTER IV

Brother Russell, Aunt Fannie Barber and Other Singing Friends

From nineteen-and-four until about 1914 or '15 or even later, there were quite a few songs about the railroad. It was sort of like the era when cowboy songs were popular, which was earlier. You see the railroads were building and there were just lots of railroad songs. Back then there were train wrecks like there are car wrecks now. Fast cars now—that's what the kids say "sends" people—but then it was trains. Before that it must have been horses, and that's maybe why cowboy songs were popular—from the 1870's on. To be a cowboy or an engineer was a sort of a hero. From about 1910 to 1912 I was very much of a fan of the railroads. They represented all romance. I was about twelve at the time. A lot of these I sing—I remember lot of the railroad songs, too—were just popular songs back then, like "Jim Blake," and "Casey Jones," and "The Wreck of the old Ninety-seven."

There's one that I still like to sing, which was taught to me by my old friend, Brother F. M. Russell. It was about the same wreck as this song, "The Wreck of Number Nine," was written, but this was called "Al Bowen." As far as I know, Brother Russell and I are the only ones that sing that song, because Al Bowen's sister wrote this ballad, and I've never seen anyone else who sang the song. It was just a family ballad that she'd written out. The wreck happened in Illinois, and Brother Russell was born and raised in Illinois near there. And he learned this song from Al Bowen's sister.

AL BOWEN

'Twas Christmas Eve and the night so dark
That the moon had hidden her face;
Al Bowen, a faithful engineer,
Went faithfully to his place.

Al had a smile, kind word for all;
A courteous man was he.
His winning ways made many friends
Many will agree.

Before he made his fatal trip,
He cheerfully proclaimed,
"Goodbye, mother dear, if I don't come home,
Know I love you all the same."

"I hate to make my run tonight,
My headlights are no good;
And I fear some evil may take place;
I feel just like it would."

"There's no use to be afraid,
No extra men have we;
I will do my duty, let come what may;
What is to be I must be."

He took his seat inside the cab,
McNeely by his side.
"Keep your seat, old boy," he said,
"We'll take a flying ride."

"We're thirty minutes late tonight,
Buchanan going to swear;
He's switching now at the station, Bob,
I see his headlight there."

"Pile in more coal, heat 'er up," he said,
"We're going to make up that time."
To his surprise he saw a headlight,
Come streaming straight down the line.

"That's old Number Nine, good God!" he said,
"And she's already 'round the neck.
Oh, jump, Mac, jump; I'll stay with 'er.
You'll find me in the wreck."

The iron steeds met with an awful crash
And bursting like a shell,
The roaring flames and scalding steams
Made it an awful Hell.

But Christmas morning the searchers came
And found the bodies there;
But the souls of the engineers had flown
To Elysian fields so fair.

And we'll never know the cause of it,
A signal wrong was given.
But this we know, they're at rest
In a far away peaceful Heaven.

I love songs that I can get histories on and that tie in together. I always loved "The Wreck of the Number Nine." Then when I heard "Al Bowen"—which was years later—I was really happy to get that. Brother Russell told me that happened back there in Illinois, and he gave me a picture of the station there at Katy.

Brother Russell is an old Baptist minister who is now about eighty-five or eighty-six years old. He was born and raiᶜed there in Illinois, but came here to Arkansas when he was a young man. He was a good friend to my husband and I, and he has remained a good friend ever since. He was a good singer and a good teacher and was also a good pianist. In fact, he was the best *educated* fiddler I've ever known—he played by note and taught it. And naturally, whenever he would come visiting, we'd have music and singing and he taught me some songs that I still sing today. Like this "Merrimac at Sea"—I can remember him visiting with us in the summer of 1920 and teaching me this song; since then I've seen and heard lots of other versions, but this is the one I've always sung since then.

MERRIMAC AT SEA

I will sing you a song of the *Merrimac* at sea,
A fine large ship was she.
While sailing in route to New Orleans
She sank to the bottom of the sea.

> *Chorus:*
> Oh, the sea how it roars, how it roars,
> The stormy wind how it blows,
> While tossed a poor sailor to and fro,
> And the ladies were all down below.

First one that came in was the captain of the ship,
And a fine looking fellow was he.
Saying, "I have a wife in New Orleans
And tonight she's a-looking for me."

"She may gaze, she may look with her beautiful eyes,
She may look to the bottom of the sea.
She may look for me but I'll not return
And tomorrow she'll a widow be."

> *Chorus:*

Next one that came in was a little cabin boy
A fine little fellow was he.
Saying, "I have a mother in New Orleans
And tonight she's a-looking for me."

"She may gaze, she may look with her beautiful eyes,
She may look to the bottom of the sea.
She may look for me but I'll not return
And tomorrow she will childless be."

    Chorus:

Next one that came in was a greasy old cook
A greasy old fellow was he.
Saying, "I care more for my pot, kettle
And hook than I do for the roaring of the sea."

    Chorus:

Around and around, three times around
And she sank to the bottom of the sea,
And tonight they can look for her return
But tonight on the bottom she will be.

    Chorus:

Elder Russell had a good sense of humor and knew a number
of these comic songs. Now, I don't sing them much, but one that
I remember him singing was this "Restless Night," which as a
matter of fact I have recorded.

A RESTLESS NIGHT

Come all you good people, I pray you draw near,
A comical ditty you shortly shall hear;
A comical story to you I'll unfold,
I went to Missouri when twenty years old.
    Down, down, derry down, down.
    Down, down, derry down, down.

I stopped at a tavern to stay all night;
The supper and breakfast I thought was all right.
The table was set and the knick-knacks were spread,
'Twas hoe cake and hominy and possum head.
    Down, down, derry down, down.
    Down, down, derry down, down.

And after these people were heartily fed
On hoe cake and hominy and possum head;
The pallet was made, the sheepskins were spread,
"And, now," said the old man, "we'll all go to bed."
    Down, down, derry down, down.
    Down, down, derry down, down.

I laid myself down expecting some ease,
But scarcely could rest for the lice and the fleas;
The lice they would bite and the fleas they would crawl,
'Twas enough to torment any human at all.
    Down, down, derry down, down.
    Down, down, derry down, down.

I kicked and I cuffed and I fought them all night;
I scarcely could scratch as fast as they'd bite;
The roughest entertainment that ever I saw,
Was lying on a pallet of sheepskin and straw.
    Down, down, derry down, down.
    Down, down, derry down, down.

Adieu to Missouri, I bid you farewell;
I go back to Arkansas where I used to dwell;
Where the ladies were raring and tearing their hair
For the loss of their lover when I left them there.
> Down, down, derry down, down.
> Down, down, derry down, down.

Elder Russell was just one of many friends of the family who taught me songs. There were many, especially in my childhood, for I learned 90 percent of my songs by the time I was eighteen. One I remember most clearly was Aunt Fanny Barber. I used to go over and stay with her. She had to stay alone quite a bit, and she'd have me to come over to stay with her when her husband was gone. For two or three days . . . I was a little girl . . . just for company. She's been dead for close to fifty years. She lived about a mile away, I guess. We didn't live in town, we lived out in the country, what's now known as west of Pangburn. We were in Cleburne County and Pangburn is in White County, but the line was near. She lived out in the country where I was born and raised. She was a very nice old farm woman.

Aunt Fanny, she used to pick cotton. They had a small patch of cotton and we used to go out in the cotton patch and I picked cotton with them and she'd sing me songs while we were picking cotton. I can just see her out there singing "Barbara Allen." She had one daughter (she had several sons, I don't remember how many) but she had that one daughter and she named her Barbara. And she had died when she was about fourteen. And Aunt Fanny'd sing me this song and I can see the old thing with tears dripping down her cheeks. She said she had sung the song since she was a girl and named her only girl child Barbara because of the song "Barbara Allen." She taught me the song—I first heard it from Aunt Fanny Barber.

BARBARA ALLEN

'Twas all in the merry, merry month of May
And the green buds all a-swellin',
When young Sir James on a deathbed lay
For the love of Barbara Allen.

Then he sent his man unto her then
To the town where she was a-dwellin';
Saying, "My master's sick, and he sent for you,
If your name be Barbara Allen."

Well, slowly, slowly rose she up,
And so slowly she came a-nigh him.
And all she said when thus she came,
"Young man, I think you are dying."

Then he turned his pale face to her then,
Oh, death was on him a-dwellin'.
"Oh, Barbry dear, won't you pity me,
For I'm on my deathbed lyin' "

"Well, if on your deathbed you now lie,
Then death is in you a-dwellin',
And better, I'm sure, that you never will be,
For you can't have Barbara Allen."

"Do you remember down in Scarlet Town,
When the wine was freely flowin',
You toasted the ladies all around,
But you slighted Barbara Allen."

"I do remember in yonder town,
And the wine was freely a-flowin',
And I toasted the fair ladies all around,
But my heart loved Barbara Allen."

Then he turned his pale face to the wall,
And death was with him a-dealin'.
"Farewell, farewell, my dear friends all,
Farewell, my Barbara Allen."

And while she was walking 'cross the fields,
She spied his corpse a-coming.
"Let down, let down," she said to them,
"That I may look upon him."

Then she looked upon his pale dead face,
Her cheeks with laughter a-swellin'.
'Til then her friends cried, "Oh, away,
'Tis unworthy Barbara Allen."

But on her deathbed where she lay,
She begged to be buried by him,
And thus repented of the day,
That in life she had denied him.

"Go make my bed, my mother dear,
And make it straight and narrow.
For Sir James has died on the yesterday,
And that I for him tomorrow."

Sir James was buried on a Saturday night,
And Barbry died on the Sunday.
And the mother died with grief for both,
And was buried on a Easter Monday.

Aunt Fanny and I often went to church together. We went to the same church and I always sat next to Aunt Fanny and we sang together. And so when we'd sing together at home or out picking cotton, we'd often sing the old hymns, and songs like that and those are the songs that I most associate with Aunt Fanny. Like this "Old Churchyard" which is *still* one of my favorites.

THE OLD CHURCH YARD

Oh come, come with me to the old churchyard,
I will know all the paths through the old greensward.
Friends are sleeping out there who we want to regard,
Let us trace out their names in the old churchyard.
Oh, weep not for them, their sorrows are o'er.
Oh, why weep for friends when they'll weep no more?
Oh, sweet is that sleep in the cold and the hard,
Yet their pillows may be in the old churchyard.

I know that it's vain when our friends depart,
To breathe kind words to a breaking heart.
I know that the joy of life is marred,
When we follow those friends to the old churchyard.
But when I'm asleep beneath yonder tree,
Oh, please do not weep, dear friend, for me.
I'm so weary, so way-worn, why retard
That peace that I seek in the old churchyard?

They are sleeping out there in sweet repose,
Released from the world's sad bereavement and woes.
And who would not rest with the friends they regard,
In quiet and peace in the old churchyard?
We'll rest in the hope of that great day,
When beauty will spring from these prisons of clay,
When old Gabriel's trump and the voice of the Lord
Will awake all the dead in the old churchyard.

Now, if you notice, many of the old hymns glorify the peace of death. Maybe the times were just hard and I think maybe people had a brighter hope in eternity. I believe they believed more firmly in eternity than many do now. I tell you, when you get old enough and tired enough and suffer enough, it brings relief. As long as I can get around with a stick and somebody helping me onto a plane and go on and be with young folks, and still can hear singing, why then I'm not looking forward to death. But shut me up in a place—a nursing home somewhere where I couldn't take care of myself, where I couldn't associate with anybody, only those that were just as old and infirm and as full of pills and pains as I was, and I think I might look forward to the release of it, too.

Now, I had this experience. I went down to this old churchyard at Good Springs, and I walked through there and I found many of the people that I didn't know where they were, right there on the tombstones. There was Aunt Fanny, and, oh, there were dozens that I didn't even know where they were. I knew *she* was dead, but there were many others of my age and a little older than I. It was a nice cool place to sit down and to drink out of the old spring. And I really did get a feeling for death's peace. And I'd like to go back and visit and walk through there. And I think whoever it was that wrote this song—"The Lone Pilgrim" —that he was thinking of that kind of peace and quiet. "The Lone Pilgrim" or "The White Pilgrim," it's the same thing.

THE LONE PILGRIM

I came to the place where the lone pilgrim lay
And I silently stood by the tomb,
And in a low whisper I heard something say,
"Oh, how sweetly asleep here alone."

The tempest can howl and the loud thunders roll,
And gathering storms may arise,
But calm is my feeling, at rest is my soul,
The tears are all wiped from my eyes.

The calls from my Master compelled me from home.
I bid my companions farewell.
I kissed my dear children who now for me mourn.
In far distant regions they dwell.

I wandered in exile, a stranger abroad,
No friend and no relatives nigh.
I met with contagion and sank to the tomb;
My soul flew to mansions on high.

Go and tell my companions and children most dear,
To weep not for me, I am gone.
And the same man that led me through trials severe,
Has kindly assisted me home.

For the lightning may flash and the loud thunders roll,
And gathering storms may arise.
Still calm is my feeling, at rest is my soul,
The tears are all wiped from my eyes.

America was settled by pilgrims. A pilgrim is someone that—if I understand the meaning of the word—a pilgrim protested against this one church that they had there, and for religious freedom they went on someplace else. Now I've heard many say that they thought this lone pilgrim was probably one of those early people in America. Now that "white" pilgrim, I think somebody stuck that to it. I think in the beginning it was called "The Lone Pilgrim." You wouldn't have to be white to be a pilgrim. We have black pilgrims now, that are protesting and fighting for their freedom just as we had to. But a pilgrim is someone who is on a journey—a religious person going to some shrine or something like that—going somewhere because of what he believes.

You know, there are two things in life we do alone—birth and death—we're alone. Our mother can help us just so far in birth—a mother can bear a child, bring it into the world, but she just cannot take that breath of life for you. That's something that we have to do for ourselves. And when this breath leaves us, we also go by ourselves. In birth and death, we're always alone.

And in life, isn't there always one side of us that we feel nobody ever understands? In this we are a stranger to even our very best loved one. Maybe this is why I love songs like this, especially that one "The Wayfaring Stranger" that Aunt Fanny Barber and I used to sing.

THE WAYFARING STRANGER

I'm just a poor wayfaring stranger,
I'm traveling through a world of woe.
But there's no sickness, toil or danger,
In that bright land to which I go.
I'm going there to see my mother,
She said she'd meet me when I come.
Oh, I'm just going over Jordan,
I'm only going over home.

I know dark clouds gonna gather around me,
I know my way'll be rough and steep.
But beautiful fields lie just before me
Where God's redeemed, their vigils keep.
I'm going there to see my classmates,
They've all gone on, now, one by one.
Oh, I'm just going over Jordan,
I'm only going over home.

I want to wear a crown of glory,
When I get home to that good land.
But I'd rather sing redemption's story
In concert with an angel band.
I'm going there to see my Savior.
I dwell with him, no more to roam.
I'm only going over Jordan,
I'm only going over home.

I'll soon be done with earthly trials,
Oh, soon I'll rest in the old churchyard.
I'll drop this cross of self-denial,
Then I'll go singing home to God.
I'm going there to see my loved ones
Who've gone before me one by one.
I'm only going over Jordan,
Oh, I'm just going over home.

Aunt Fanny was just an old lady that had no children. Her children were married off, as mine are now. She was elderly and she didn't like to be alone, and she would get me to go and stay these nights when her husband was gone. He was a mail carrier, I think. I loved her like a grandmother. You see, I never had a grandmother. Both of my grandmothers died before I was born, and Aunt Fanny Barber was the closest to a grandmother I ever had. She was just a neighbor. I don't know, there was something even as a child, I always loved elderly people. Now since I've gotten old and full of pills and pains, I'd rather be with younger people. (Maybe I've never liked my own age group.)

I love elderly people still, especially if they've got courage enough. I don't like complainers. I can have lots of sympathy for you, if you don't have too much for yourself. But I consider that self-pity is the most destructive thing we've ever indulged in. I never allow myself to be sorry for myself. And I just don't like to see people be sorry for themselves. It's too destructive.

There was another old neighbor lady, too, that I just loved, Aunt Sally Bittle. She lived alone, just as I do now. She was an old widow woman and she got lonely, and I'd invite her over to spend the night.

Back in those days our bedrooms were scarce, and my sister and I slept together. I always slept with Aunt Sally. She had epilepsy and my sister was scared of that, so she would sleep on the floor. And I always got the bedroom and this big featherbed—great big featherbed that we had. Now she's the one, Aunt Sally Bittle, who taught me "The Orphan Girl" and I loved it then and I still do. I think it's one of the most beautiful ballads I've heard.

THE ORPHAN GIRL

"No home, no home," said an orphan girl
At the door of a princely hall.
As she trembling stood on the marble steps
And leaned on the marble wall.

"Oh, give me a place out of this cold wind,
Just a place to sleep," she said.
"A pallet in the corner will do for me,
But give me a piece of bread."

But the rich man shook his stately head
And he slammed his mansion door.
His proud lips curled with scorn as he said,
"No room and no bread for the poor."

"I must freeze," she sobbed, and sank on the steps
And tried to cover her feet,
With her ragged dress all tattered and torn
And covered with snow and sleet.

The rich man lay on his couch of down
And dreamed of his silver and gold,
While the little girl lay in the snow on the steps
And murmured, "So cold, so cold."

The night rolled on and the midnight chimes
Rang out like a funeral knell.
The earth was wrapped in a winding sheet
And blinding snow still fell.

Next morning when the sun arose
The poor little girl lay dead at the rich man's door,
But her soul had fled to her mother and dad,
Where there's room and bread for the poor.

And the rich man still lay on his couch of down
But his soul, too, had fled.
Now I can't know where rich men go,
But I do know the rich man is dead.

Aunt Sally Bittle sang many songs, but this was one that until I heard her sing it I had never known.

Now, if you ask around here about singers, you'll hear that the Starks were the very best, especially Uncle Bob Starks. He and my father were really the best singers in this area I think, and I can well remember Uncle Bob's big voice coming from church above all the other singers on a Sunday, or just singing as he walked down the road. I have a recording of Uncle Bob before he died not so many years ago.

Two of my sisters married two of the Starks boys. They were brothers, and both nephews of Uncle Bob. One of them, Louis, was a favorite of mine, and still is for that matter. He was a very good ballad singer and fiddler, in fact, a professional. He went out to California and was known all throughout there as "Arkie and His Hillbillies." He was Arkie—he just took that stage name for himself when he went out there. We just loved to get together and he would play his fiddle and we would sing together. We could go on for an hour just on one song like "Rye Whiskey." One time while he and I were sitting around we took this song "Mandy" and made up some new verses for it, and when he went to California, he and his Hillbillies used to sing it—back in the '40's, from about '35 until '50 sometime, I guess.

MANDY

I don't want to steal or rob,
But I'm out of a job,
And my Mandy keeps on nagging all the time, time, time.
My Mandy keeps on nagging all the time.

Oh, time's is hard,
If I had some lard,
I'd keep my skillet greasy all the time, time, time.
Keep my skillet greasy all the time.

Time's is rough,
If I had some snuff,
I'd keep my Mandy dipping all the time, time, time.
For Mandy keeps on nagging all the time.

Oh, times are risky,
If I had some whiskey,
I would make my Mandy boozy all the time, time time.
I'd keep her good and boozy all the time.

Honey, if you say so,
We won't work no more,
We'll just lay 'round your pappy's all the time, time, time.
We'll lay 'round your pappy's all the time.

Oh, 'times I'se lazy,
If I had me some greasy,
I would keep my taters frying all the time, time, time.
I'd keep my taters frying all the time.

You can make up all the verses you want to. Uncle Dave Macon used to sing that "Grease Your Skillet." Louis was some eight years younger than I was. He married my baby sister. He still lives in California. Well, he was a very fine fiddler and banjo player, just played anything. But I think he told me that he hadn't picked up a fiddle in ten years when I saw him last.

When I was eleven years old—that was our last year at home out over Pangburn—there was this little boy about my age that loved singing as much as I do—Emerson Pickens. At that time, my mother took this paper, published in Memphis, the *Commercial Appeal*. This story was written as news and then this ballad was printed later—someone had made it and sent it in. Emerson first found it and he showed it to me. It had no tune, but we couldn't leave a thing like that go by without singing it. So he and I sat down and figured out our tune . . . we put a tune to it *soon.* You take kids as full of singing as we were, eleven years old, we could make a tune in a few minutes if we wanted to sing— and we wanted to sing this.

The story actually happened, of this man who came to the gallows and was to be hung. It actually happened. The story gave his name but I've forgotten it, but he was a close friend of Allen Bain, and they had gone hunting, and he came back and Bain went on someplace else on his horse. And when he got back, Bain didn't turn up at all, so Bain's family had him arrested for murder. They had had a quarrel but made it up, and went hunting together. And they said he had murdered Bain and he was convicted on circumstantial evidence. This was supposed to have happened someplace in Tennessee.

ALLEN BAIN

They are taking me to the gallows, Mother,
They mean to hang me there.
The drop will fall beneath my feet
And leave me in the air.
From me is gone each earthly joy
And from me fled each hope;
They'll pull over my face a long black cap
Around my neck a rope.
They think I've murdered Allen Bain,
And so the judge has said
To hang me on the gallows, Mother,
And hang me till I'm dead.

The birds that sing on yonder hill,
Those lambs that skip and play
Are clear and pure of human blood
And, Mother, so am I.
Yet twelve good men have found me guilty
Guilty of bloodshed.
So they'll hang me to the gallows, Mother,
And hang me till I'm dead.

Lay me not down by my father's side
For once I mind he said,
"No child that stains my spotless name
Shall share my immortal bed."
And when there by his side I slept
In my narrow bed of clay,
His frowning skull and crumbling bones
Would shrink from me away.
For, Mother, I'm a stain upon his name
Though I'm innocent of bloodshed
Still they will hang me on the gallows, Mother,
And hang me till I'm dead.

Place me in my coffin, Mother,
As you've sometimes seen me rest
With one hand beneath my head
The other one on my breast.
Place my Bible near my heart
Poor Mother, do not weep
But kiss me as in happier days
You'd kiss me when asleep,
For, Mother, then I'll be at rest
For I'm innocent of bloodshed,
Yet they'll hang me to the gallows, Mother
And hang me till I'm dead.

And for the rest do as you please
And little do I reck
But cover up that cursed stain,
That black mark round my neck.
For, Mother, unjustly they put it there
I'm innocent as I've said,
But they'll hang me to the gallows, Mother,
And hang me till I'm dead.

Then a horsemen appeared with a lathered steed
And tightly gathered reins.
He sits erect, he waves his hand,
"Good God, it's Allen Bain!"
Now, Mother, praise the God you serve
And raise your drooping head
For this murderous gallows black and grim
Is cheated of its dead.

You just don't know what's going on in the mind of a child—what a child will like in a children's song. So, I believe that at least with my children, I just exposed them to anything I wanted to sing and then let them choose when I rocked them all to sleep. Every grandchild that I have, I rocked to sleep until they were two or three years old, until the next baby came along. When their nap time came, Granny always got them to sleep. And I'd put the bigger one on a pallet and I've had those four of Clinton's, all four of them laying out. Brenda, I guess, was about eight when the last one was born. But she'd come in and sit at the window after dinner, and they'd all take a nap, the little ones. And I'd just ask them what they wanted me to sing. And whatever they wanted me to sing, I sang. Sometimes they'd go to sleep to "The Red-Headed Stranger," sometimes it was "Jesse James." Sometimes it *was* a child's song. But mostly that "House Carpenter's Wife" has been a classic in my family. And this "Allen Bain." Sandra now, she never would go to sleep for anything other than "Allen Bain." She has almost worn out two records I have on "Allen Bain," so you don't know what a child . . .

I sing my children whatever they ask to be sung. My eldest granddaughter, my first grandchild, Erma Dene, of all the things that she liked best—there was this one song that she'd especially always want when she was about four, that she'd ask me to sing this old thing, "Don't Go Out Tonight, My Darling."

DON'T GO OUT TONIGHT, MY DARLING

Don't go out tonight, my darling,
Oh, please don't leave me here alone.
Stay here at home with me, my darling,
I am so lonely when you're gone.

Now your friends may be jolly,
And the wine may flow so free.
Yet I'll do my best to entertain you,
If you will only stay with me.

Now, alas, he's gone and left me,
With a curse upon his lips.
And no one knows what I have suffered,
Oh, that awful cup he sips.

Now they brought me home my husband;
There's heavy footsteps on the floor.
Yes, they have brought me home my darling,
He's lying dead upon the floor.

She was four years old. She'd come down there and immediately she'd ask me just as quick as she came. And she'd just sit there and the tears would just pour down her cheeks. Then she'd wipe them and blow her nose. And so, one day she came in and she asked me to sing and I said, "I'll sing 'Froggie Went A-Courting,'" and she said, "I hate it. I don't want 'Froggie Went A-Courting.' It's silly." And I mentioned everything that I thought would entertain her. No, she wanted this "Don't Go Out Tonight, My Darling." And I said, "Erma Dene, I can't do that."

"Why?"

"Well, you just sit there and weep and cry. Honey, I don't want to do it." She said, "Granny, I just love to feel that way." She said, "I'd rather feel that way as any way I know." Well, you see it was tears of enjoyment. And there's songs that I weep with when somebody sings them. If you love serious things when you get older, chances are you do while you're a child.

This "Allen Bain" and the "Blind Child's Prayer" are the only two songs I can ever remember clipping from the newspaper. I *did* have a poetry book, now, with things from poetry columns in a paper. And, as a matter of fact, I also got "Little Jim," which I sing, from there. But I think those are the only three. And that poetry book was blown away with all of my ballets.

LITTLE JIM

The night was dark and stormy,
The wind was howling wild.
A patient mother watched beside
The deathbed of her child.
A little wornout creature,
His once bright eyes growing dim;
It was a coaler's wife and child,
They called him Little Jim.

And, oh, to see those briny tears
Fast hurrying down her cheeks;
She kneels to offer up a prayer
But is afraid to speak.
Lest she might wake the son
She loves far better than her life,
For she has all a mother's love
Has that poor coaler's wife.

Uplifted hands and so she kneels
Beside the sick child's bed.
She prayed, "O God, please spare my son
And take my life instead."
She gets her answer from the boy,
Softly falls the words from him,
"Oh, Mother, angels do so smile
And beckon Little Jim."

"I have no pain, dear Mother, now,
But I am, oh, so dry,
Just give poor Jim another drink
And, Mother, please don't cry.
Tell Father when he comes from work
I said 'good night' to him
And now I think I'll go to sleep."
'Twas the last from Little Jim.

The door is softly opened,
The coaler's step is heard;
The father and mother meet again
But neither speaks a word.
He knew that all was over,
Yes, knew his son was dead;
He took the candle in his hand
And walks toward the bed.

His trembling lips give token
Of grief he tries to conceal;
Now, see, his wife has gained him,
The stricken couple kneel.
With heart bowed in sadness,
They humbly ask of Him
In heaven that they may meet again
Their own poor Little Jim.

"Little Jim" I wanted to sing so bad—we lived over on the mountain then—that I just clipped the words and put it to my own tune, and since then I've always sung it. And I've never heard anyone else sing it. I doubt if it was a song. It probably was just a poem somebody wrote—just a poem in a paper, and I don't even know what paper. That was before "Allen Bain." I was about eight years old. But I didn't have to bluff that time. I could read it. I had a *very* good teacher, my mother, who saw to it that I could read at an early age. She taught me to read by flatly quitting and refusing to read things to me—she'd only tell me words. I'd learn things by heart at school—the First Reader—but I wasn't reading. It was like that "Blind Child's Prayer" business, trying to fool people. I didn't even know my letters. When it came to things I wanted to read, papers and songs and things, I naturally couldn't. So my mother bought me some books with children's stories—"Sleeping Beauty" was one—and she wouldn't read it to me. She told me some words, that's all. Made me tell the letters for it. And I got so frustrated I just had to learn to read. If she hadn't done that, I'd still not know how to read, because I could memorize anything—I still can.

Now, if I disliked a song, I'd probably have to work at it to learn it. If I liked it—something like finding this version I did of the "Four Marys," what I'd had in my mind trying to dig it out of this tired brain of mine and out of the past for a long time—then once I found this, it all came back and I can think of nothing else for maybe weeks but that. And then I couldn't forget it if I wanted to.

I remember one time we were picking cotton—as a child I was in the cotton patch—I think I was seven years old at the time and I'd first heard this "No Telephone in Heaven," and I

NO TELEPHONE IN HEAVEN

sang it over and over all day long. I couldn't think of anything else until finally a man offered me a quarter. Now, a quarter at that time—as a child twenty-five cents meant as much as a dollar and a half would mean to a child now. Well, this man, he gave me twenty-five cents if I would please just not sing "No Telephone in Heaven" again that day. And the next day I could sing it all I wanted to.

"Now I can't fool with baby," the smiling virgin said.
She stopped and gently toyed with the golden curly head.
"I want to call up Mama," came the answer full and free,
"Will you telephone and ask her when she's coming home to me?"
>   *Chorus:*
>   "My child," the virgin murmured, as she stroked the anxious brow;
>   "We've no telephone connections where your mother lives at now."
>   "No telephones in Heaven," and the tears sprang in her eyes;
>   "And I thought God had everything with him up in the skies."

"Tell her to come to baby because I am afraid
With no one here to kiss me when the lights begin to fade.
Tell her I get so lonesome I don't know what to do,
And Father cries so much, I guess he must be lonesome, too."
>   *Chorus:*

"Alone here I have wandered since Mama went away.
My dolly's clothes all ragged, she gets thinner every day
Tell her to come and fix it for, since she went away,
My poor little lonesome dolly gets thinner every day."
>   *Chorus:*

Now that song, that's just a popular song of the day, not what I call a classic. A classic ballad is something you class highly, something in your idea. Maybe what someone else would call a classic I wouldn't. "Lady Margaret," a nice version of it, I think that's a classic. This "Four Marys" I consider that one too—to me, maybe not to you. And a variant of this "Hangman's Tree" that is very old—I found this back in about, I believe, in about the fifteenth century in an old Scottish book. And almost this version. Almost exactly like this is, and I'd been singing it then for forty years.

HANGMAN ON THE GALLOWS TREE

"Oh, hangman, hangman, loosen up the line,
I see my mother a-coming from our far-off distant home."

"Oh, Mother, my Mother, and have you brought me gold
Or have you paid my fee?
Or did you come to see your only son
Hangin' high on a gallows tree?"

"Oh no, son, no and I have brought no gold,
Nor have I paid your fee;
For I am come to see an unworthy son
Hangin' high on a gallows tree."

"Oh, hangman, hangman, loosen up your line,
For I see my father a-coming from our far-off distant home."

"Oh, Father, my Father, and have you brought me gold
Or have you paid my fee?
Or did you come to see your only son
Hangin' high on a gallows tree?"

"Oh no, son, no and I have brought no gold,
Nor have I paid your fee;
For I am come to see an unworthy son
Hangin' high on a gallows tree."

"Oh, slackman, slackman, slacken up the line,
I see my sister a-coming from a far-off distant shore."

"Oh, Sister, my Sister, and have you brought me gold
Or did you pay my fee?
Or did you come to see your brother hung,
Hangin' high on a gallows tree?"

"Oh no, sir, no and I brought no gold,
Nor did I pay your fee;
Alas, I but came to see my brother hung,
Hangin' high on a gallows tree."

"Oh, slackman, slackman, slacken up your line;
I see my sweetheart coming from a far-off distant shore."

"Oh, Sweetheart, my Sweetheart, have you brought me gold
Or have you paid my fee?
Or did you come to see me hung,
Hangin' high on a gallows tree."

"Oh yes, dear, yes dear, I have brought you gold
And I have paid your fee;
I never intended to see my love hung,
Hangin' high on a gallows tree."

But I don't think the age has everything to do with a classic. You might write a classic. Something that would be classical—would teach something, be worth preserving. It could be dirty and old and trash and not teach anything and be a thousand years old and still would be that when it started out. That's what the word "classic" to me means. That teaches something that's worth remembering, that's worth passing on. That song, it does teach. Well, if we want to go back to the Bible, you see, God said that a man would forsake father and mother and sister and brother and cleave to his wife. And the twain would be one flesh. I think that's what this is teaching, this old hangman here. His father didn't pay him out and his sister didn't pay him out, and one version I read one time, he also had a brother and he didn't pay him out. But his sweetheart did.

Nearly all the songs I sing have stories to them. I don't care a thing in this world—or hardly a thing—for a song that doesn't tell a story or teach a lesson. The only way I could ever really learn history was to get it in a story. Dates I don't remember. And I guess the same is true with songs. Things I'm not interested in, I close 'em off and forget 'em.

Now there are some songs which don't tell a story that I do sing, like hymns, but they *teach* something. Or they tell our experiences, our feelings—many hymns will do that. Like this one "How Tedious and Tasteless the Hours"—that has been such a comfort to me through the years. It tells no story, yet I love the song. It runs along with my experience. Sometimes we feel as Elijah did, we are out there on the mountain all alone and they've killed them all but us. Everybody has that feeling sometime. We feel alone, and then we feel the presence of the Higher Power, God.

HOW TEDIOUS AND TASTELESS THE HOURS

How tedious and tasteless the hours,
When Jesus no longer I see!
Sweet prospects, sweet birds, and sweet flow'rs
Have all lost their sweetness to me.
The mid-summer sun shines but dim,
The fields strive in vain to look gay.
But when I am happy in Him,
December's as pleasant as May.

His name yields the richest perfume,
And sweeter than music His voice;
His presence disperses my gloom,
And makes all within me rejoice;
I should, were He always thus nigh,
Have nothing to wish or to fear;
No mortal so happy as I,
My summer could last all the year.

Content with holding His face,
My all to His pleasure resigned,
No changes of season or place
Would make any change in my mind!
While blessed with a sense of His love,
A palace a toy would appear;
And prisons would palaces prove,
If Jesus would dwell with me there.

But these ballads, I don't know why I feel so strong with them, since nothing like the stories they tell would ever happen to me personally . . . but I do love them. Like this "Lady Margaret" business with the king's son—I couldn't identify with that in personal experience. But since the first I heard that song, I've had a feeling of compassion for Lady Margaret. These things tell in ourselves.

And I guess bringing up compassion is like teaching us, at least about ourselves. A ballad can teach something, too, and that is important. Now, this "Lady Gay"—my mother sang that, so it is especially dear to me for that reason—but it does teach that you shouldn't grieve overlong. At best it's useless. We can never return to the past and it's best to bury the past . . . then not let our tears rot the winding sheet.

LITTLE LADY GAY

There was a little lady, a little lady gay,
And children she had three.
She sent them off to the north summeree
To learn their grammaree.

They hadn't been gone but about three weeks,
I'm sure it was not four,
When sweet Death came over the land
And swept those babes away.

Oh, what do you reckon their mother will say
When she does hear the news.
She'll cry aloud and wring her hands,
"Where is my three little babes?"

Christmas times were drawing near,
And the wind blew loud and cold.
Those three little babes came flying down
All in their mother's room.

The table was set and a cloth spread on,
'Twas set with bread and wine.
"Come eat and drink, my three little babes,
Come eat and drink of mine."

"We cannot eat your bread, dear Mother,
We cannot drink your wine,
For yonder stands our own dear Savior,
Just waiting for our return."

The bed was fixed in the finest room
And a golden sheet spread on.
"Lie there, lie there, my three little babes
'Til in the morning soon."

"We cannot sleep in your bed, dear Mother,
'Til in the morning soon,
For yonder stands our own dear Savior,
Just waiting for our return."

The oldest said to the youngest one,
"It will soon be time we're gone,
For there He stands with outstretched hand
Waiting for our return."

Then wings were spread and away they flew
All from their mother's room.
Her three little babes in Heaven will be
All in the morning soon.

Now, I never felt, even when I was a child, that those boys came back as ghosts. They came back in a dream. I know from reading and talking with other folks around here that some feel that there are witchcraft and ghosts involved in this song. But I still feel as I did as a child on "Lady Gay" to get something from the ballad.

These boys came back in her *dream* and refused to eat her bread and drink her wine and sleep in her bed, for she was disturbing their rest. We could have a dream like that even now. It's possible. She cried so much that the grave became so wet that it wet the winding sheet. People away back, they were only wrapped in a sheet and buried in the earth, I've been told. As a matter of fact, I knew an old lady one time that told me that she didn't want to be put in a box to be buried. That she was of the earth, and the Scripture said that she'd return to the earth. And so when she died, wanted to be wrapped in a winding sheet and let Mother Earth enfold her in her soft arms, and not to have to lay there and be eaten of worms in a box.

CHAPTER V

Children's Songs and Classics

Now, it's scarcely ever, if you sing a song from memory, that you'll sing it exactly word for word each time. You'll probably change a word here and there, which keeps it changing. This is true of all songs, the classic songs and other kinds. Well, "Go Tell Aunt Nancy" is not a classic; it's my own version. Most of it I wrote . . . for the kids, and just to sing it to them. That thing, if I want to play around with it, it's all right; but "The House Carpenter's Wife," now I count that one of the classics. That's truly a folksong. And I don't change it. This arrangement of mine, I never heard of it except we kids just made it up, and sang it along as a child. Probably it's not any more authentic than I am.

There *is* a very old version that the walnut killed the goose. That's right, because years ago I found that. I don't remember what collection it was in, but about thirty or forty years ago I found that in an old collection of folksongs. I'd been singing it since I was a kid as Aunt Nancy and the walnut—down came the walnut—we find the grey goose that died in the millpond and I heard that. I think we sang that some, but not much. I always preferred "Go Tell Aunt Nancy."

The first of that I heard was as a child. A little girl, Merty Cowan, sang that. I was very small, first school. And then my mother sang some verses of this. I guess the original is really the old goose who was always in the millpond. But I've always sung where she was killed by a walnut, definitely—the walnut hit her on the top of the head and killed her. Aunt *Nancy's* goose, and I remember as a child having some fierce arguments with school children over this song. Now, Merty Cowan sang it, the first time I heard it. She sang it as Aunt Nancy, and a walnut killed it. This was an older girl. I was about six, and I got it into my mind like that. Now these other verses have been picked up along the way from other children's versions of "Aunt Nancy" and from my mother's. I remember one fight I had about the way she was buried and the way that the old goose "died in the millpond,

GO TELL AUNT NANCY

standing on her head." And I said it definitely was Aunt *Rhody's* goose and not Aunt Nancy's. And so, I still say Aunt Nancy's goose was definitely killed by a walnut. She didn't die in the millpond.

And children like the way it's done now, and it's recorded like that. That's just Granny's version of "Aunt Nancy" and I think it's nobody else's. I've sung that thing so long that I don't remember where it all comes from. As a child I must have put those things in there because they're weird things. But I know that she was killed with a walnut, and she broke Granddad's teeth, and the forks, and the sawmill, and they threw her under a rock at last and buried her there. Now these things are authentic . . . the tale of it is.

Go tell Aunt Nancy, go tell Aunt Nancy,
Go tell Aunt Nancy, her old grey goose is dead.
The one that she's been saving, one that she's been saving,
The one that she's been saving, to make a feather bed.
Down come a walnut, down come a walnut,
Down come a walnut and hit her on the head.
Go tell Aunt Nancy, poor old Aunt Nancy,
Go tell Aunt Nancy the old grey goose is dead.

The gander is weeping, gander is weeping,
The gander is weeping, because his wife is dead.
Her goslings all crying, and weeping and peeping,
Her goslings all crying, their mammy they can't find.
Down come a walnut, down come a walnut,
Down come a walnut and hit her on the head.
Go tell Aunt Nancy, poor old Aunt Nancy,
Go tell Aunt Nancy her old grey goose is dead.

Go tell Aunt Nancy, go tell Aunt Nancy,
We took her in the kitchen and cooked her all day long.
And she broke all the forkteeth, broke all the forkteeth,
Broke all the forkteeth, they weren't strong enough.
Broke out Grandad's teeth, broke all Granddad's teeth,
Poor old Granddad's teeth, the old grey goose was tough.
Go tell Aunt Nancy, go tell Aunt Nancy,
Go tell Aunt Nancy that the old grey goose is tough.

Go tell Aunt Nancy, go tell Aunt Nancy,
Go tell Aunt Nancy, we hauled her to the mill.
We'll grind her into sausages or make her into mincemeat,
Grind her into sausages, if the miller only will.
She broke all the sawteeth, broke all the sawteeth,
Broke all the sawteeth, it was not strong enough.
Broke all the sawteeth, tore down the saw mill,
Broke up the circle saw, that old grey goose is tough.

Go tell Aunt Nancy, go tell Aunt Nancy,
Go tell Aunt Nancy, we know this is a shock.
But go tell Aunt Nancy, poor old Aunt Nancy,
Go tell Aunt Nancy we buried her under a rock.
Go tell Aunt Nancy, go tell Aunt Nancy,
Go tell Aunt Nancy the old grey goose is dead.
Down come a walnut, down come a walnut,
Down come a walnut and hit her on the head.

In singing a song you might not remember the exact words
you used a day or two before and if you're singing it by memory,
as long as it doesn't change the text and meaning of the song,
why it stays enough as we go along. And I might sing that tomorrow and the words might not—but the meaning wouldn't be
changed. The text of the song would never be changed; I
wouldn't do that but there might be a word here and there.
That's what makes folksongs, you see. They were handed down
from mouth to mouth and from one generation to another generation and maybe one generation didn't know exactly what the
other meant by a word that was in there, like in this "The Four
Marys" the "wee barn." I've heard that sung "the wee one"
and I've heard it sung "the baby." It doesn't change the text
any. It actually means the same in Scottish.

The words, you know, are fluid . . . they might change this way
or that, but never the meaning. I wouldn't consciously change
the words of a song, and I'd be *very* careful not to change the
meaning. But now I might sing you "Barbara Allen" today one
way, and I have at least six or eight versions of that, so tomorrow
some of this version or that might creep in. I wouldn't let it
change the actual meaning of a song, and I like to try to get the
text of the song as I originally heard it, but some of these others
might creep in there.

But with the "Four Marys" I have done this—to an audience, like of children, who wouldn't know what a "barn" is, then I would sing "wee one" instead. Really it's a "wee barn" and I studied as a child and wondered about that because I didn't know the meaning of it. A word here or there might be different like that.

Bill Monroe once told me that a true folksinger never sang a song the same way twice . . . so if they caught up on him singing it a different way, then he was a folksinger. But I think Bill was sort of half joking, because he does put in these changes without ever knowing it. I don't believe in changing my songs and neither does Bill, I know because he's very conscientious about his songs. I wouldn't willingly change even one word, but it sometimes does happen and over the centuries it happens a lot. That's why we have so many different versions. They get passed on by word of mouth from generation to generation and from century to century, some of them. You see where we have a revised version of the Bible now to make it more understood, and so it has to be with some songs, I guess. Just the words that have to be changed, not the meaning.

Now if I hear a song and it's bad English, well, that has just been corrupted. It didn't begin like that. And if it doesn't make any sense at all—which I've heard some that *did*—then that has to be changed. There's this lady I know who sings a version of "Fanny Moore." Well, there is a word, "Young Henry the *false-hearted*"; well, she puts that "sar-hearted," something like that. Well, she just misunderstood this word when she learned this song. If it's a word that's been misunderstood, yes, I'll consciously change it and put the word that was supposed to be there, to make sense. But outside of that, I don't edit old ballads, I don't fool around with them.

Now, if I want to add some verses to a children's song, something that I don't consider classic, to be left for future generations, then I could make them up out of whole cloth. And I wouldn't care if I used the old tune to it. Like with "Aunt Nancy," the big part of it, I just remembered the story of it and I change it all the time. Just put them in for the children whatever way I feel like it. But I always tell people, when I sing it or record it, that that was just my own version. That's probably no more authentic than I am in some of the verses. The *story* is as I heard it. But there's not many others that I do like that.

But now here's why I think I changed that. Because I've heard lots of versions of "Aunt Rhody" where the old goose died in the millpond but I have never felt—not even as a child—that you could drown a goose. I still don't think you could. That's why I held to this version. Even as a child I have been a stickler for basic facts and for things to make sense . . . to have reason and authenticity. You can't drown a gosling, even—I've tried it. If you turn him loose he comes out of there swimming, almost as soon as it's hatched. Well, it didn't make any sense to me, so I sing it as Merty Cowan sang it.

So you see, if some song doesn't make sense, I probably won't learn it or, if I like it, I'll change it so that it makes sense. Or I'll look for a version that makes sense. But that's about the only way I'll put myself into a song. I'm not an entertainer and never have been. Entertainers have to put too much of themselves into a song. If what I do entertains you, then I'm glad, but I never put out any effort to entertain anyone, except a few to children so I can get them to stay with me while I'm singing and the mothers are gone. Now maybe my songs entertain, but I'm not an entertainer. I've done concerts up and down the East Coast and West Coast and all through the United States, but I've never been classed an entertainer. I don't perform, you see.

The ballads I do, you're not supposed to perform them . . . let's call that traditional. A ballad, or any kind of traditional song, (especially one of what I call the classics) you have to put yourself *behind* the song. By that I mean get out of the way of it. *Present* your story, don't *perform* it. Now Elvis Presley is a performer and a good singer. But how would it look with that "twist" to "The Four Marys"? The difference between our most popular "folksingers" and me, they do perform and put too much of themselves into it. I just get behind it. I don't want any of Almeda Riddle there. Let's get the picture of Mary Hamilton, the weeping, betrayed girl, before the public. And if your ballad is good enough, it'll hold them without anything that you do. You don't have to put any tricks to your voice or anything else, if you sing it with feeling. I *do* believe a ballad should be sung with feeling and with understanding. You must feelingly present a ballad or a hymn or spiritual. Now, if you want to perform on something like "The Three Nights Drunk" or "The Black Mustache" or something like that, if the song is an entertaining song, that's all right. Go right ahead. But these others, these classics, I do feel strongly about them.

CHAPTER VI

Things That Intrigue Me
and Keep Me Busy

I've been singing for so long that there are lots of songs that I can't remember at all where I got them. Like this "Rare Willie's Drowned in Yarrow." I've tried to remember where I learned that and I can't remember, unless it was from Uncle John Wilkerson. I've just known it for a number of years. And, as a matter of fact, I had never sung the song much. My children said that they didn't ever remember hearing me sing it until the last few years. It was one of these things that I had laid aside. They had never heard me sing that "Four Marys" either. That's probably why I had to go through all that to remember it. You just don't sing four or five hundred songs every day. There's some things that they like, these I sing for them. And these that I just like, I sang them for myself, I guess. Even in concerts I haven't done this in but one or two, and that's right here in Arkansas.

RARE WILLIE DROWNED IN YARROW

Willie's fair and Willie's rare,
And Willie's wonderous bonnie.*
And Willie's promised to marry with me
If ever he married any.

The reason why I know I knew this song as a child is that I

*Granny sings it "won-der-ous." (Ed.)

remember that those lines—to marry *with* me—as a child that intrigued me very much. And then the one where her hair was so long and yellow that she tied it around his waist and she dragged it from the yarrow . . . *that* very much intrigued me.

I liked long hair. Matter of fact, because of my temper in combing my hair, I had coaxed my Dad into cutting it off when I was seven or eight years old, and then I wished it back. And I remember first thinking that—that if I had let my hair grow I might have been able to do that. My sister's hair was yellow—Claudy's, and I've always loved yellow hair. I even wished that mine would get yellow—they called it "golden" but it was yellow—but mine wouldn't ever be of that shade. And so I thought that at least if it had grown and I'd a-let it alone, it would have been long enough to tie it around somebody's waist.

> Oh, sister dear, I've dreamed a dream,
> I'm afraid it's untold sorrow;
> I dreamed I pulled the heather green
> In the darkened dens of Yarrow.
>
> Oh, sister dear, I'll read your dream,
> I'm afraid it means much sorrow;
> You'll get a letter ere it is e'en
> That your lover has drowned in Yarrow.
>
> She sought him up stream, she sought him down
> In much distress and sorrow;
> She found his body 'neath some brush
> In the darkened dens of Yarrow.
>
> Her hair it was three-quarters long,
> Its color it was yellow;
> She tied it 'round his middle small
> And pulled him out of Yarrow.
>
> My bed was made wide yestere'en
> Tonight I'll make it narrow;
> There'll never a man lie by my side
> Since Willie's drowned in Yarrow.

There's a lot of things intriguing about that song. Take this "reading" a dream, that's been since Bible days—people that thought that they could interpret dreams. I've met people that

thought they could read a dream. You know there are lots of these superstitions (like Vance Randolph has in his book), that talk about interpreting dreams.* But this I had as a child—if you dream of a wedding, you know you'll hear of a death; if you dream of a death, you'll hear of a wedding. That's folklore—and Vance Randolph has quoted my pet superstitions, too.

Now I am not superstitious, but here is a tale about someone who feels just about it as I. There was an old lady in the country. They came around and asked her about all these superstitions— she didn't believe in any superstitions whatsoever—nothing! She didn't believe in hants, she didn't believe in anything but God and Jesus Christ. And she affirmed that that was the only thing she believed in. But she said, "Brother, I'll tell you one thing. If you'll give me a good sassafras stick and ashes made from hickory wood, with a sassafras stick to stir it with and the light of the

*Ozark Superstitions. The author, Vance Randolph, had just given her a copy. (Ed.)

moon to make it, I'll make as good a lye soap as the next one."
And she said, "I'll tell you another thing. If you plant your potatoes in the light of the moon, you'll get not nary potatoes. You
better put 'em in there in the dark of the moon." So, she didn't
believe in superstitions.

Now, I couldn't tell you about the potatoes, but as a matter of
fact that business about the soap is right, because I've made soap
myself that way many times and so has anyone in these parts that's
my age anyhow. But it matters not what kind of stick or what
time of moon. I had an ash-hopper, matter of fact, even after I
was married. You dripped this water through these ashes. You
put the ashes in all the winter, you'd sprinkle them down every
once in a while. You'd put water, then more new ashes. You
kept this covered where the rains wouldn't leach it out. The
spring—generally in March or April—that was soap-making time,
because it wouldn't freeze, you know. And that made soft soap.
But then I began to buy this concentrated lye in cans—you can
still get it if you want to. You just add the lye to the grease and
it eats it up and it makes soap; it turns to soap. That's the way
soap is still made. Before we used the concentrated lye, it would
be the longer you boiled it, the stiffer it got. After something
like a year old, it got to where you could cut it down. But it was
still soft soap. And the best soap we've ever known, I think, for
washing. Whitened the clothes the best and most gentle on your
hands at the same time.

And you know the old-fashioned lye soap, they used it as a
child for many things. If you had an infection, something like
infantigo [impetigo]—"summer sores" they used to call it—there
wasn't a better remedy to first cleanse that with lye soap and then
put on your salve or whatever. This was made from ashes which
were not strong enough to eat in and irritate the flesh. It felt
soothing even to a sore—it didn't burn.

So that's right about lye soap, and often with the hickory and
the sassafras stick. Now, I said I'm not superstitious, but even I
don't start jobs on Friday. I don't believe in it, but still I don't
start long jobs on Friday. I don't mind starting a long trip or
something like that, but to put a quilt into the frames, or to quilt

it, or to begin a new top to piece it, I'd sit up until midnight Thursday night, but I wouldn't begin it on a Friday. Otherwise I'd leave it to Saturday or Monday to start it. But I'm *not* superstitious.

I've done this quilting, now, ever since I learned to sew. I learned to piece quilts so long ago that I can't remember. My mother cut the pieces and I sewed them. I've always loved to sew. Two things that I can do at once that I dearly love—that's to do hand-sewing and singing. And many's the times I've sat and sang and sewed.

I used to embroider quite a bit, and I still do crocheting—thousands upon thousands of yards of thread—but the best sewing, the thing I enjoy most, is cutting out and piecing quilts. I've pieced them by the hundreds, I believe. When they get stacked to the top of the shelf, then I give them away.

And I don't have any more idea of how many patterns I can do than how many songs I can sing. So I don't know how many patterns I've pieced—have no idea. I've pieced "Star of Bethlehem" and what they call "The Bow Tie," "The Necktie," and this "Butterfly." And "The Broken Star" and "The Lone Star," and then there's just the plain "Star." Then there's this one we call "The Seven Stars" which is seven six-pointed stars pieced into a block and then put together. There's "The Rose Garden." Any old quilter will know all of these. And I've pieced all of those, beside many others. Lot of them I don't even know their names.

Now, we took this paper, the *Kansas City Star;* my mother took that—she was an avid reader. And each week there was a quilt pattern that came out. And we clipped them, my mother and I. That was after I was grown, married, and had children. Clipped and kept these . . . and a lot of them I've done, and a lot of them I haven't. But there is everything in the quilt pattern from "The Wine Glass" to "The Coffin." I've seen them all. And most of them are pieced, not appliqued. I never pieced "The Coffin." I might be morbid, but not *that* morbid. Some old lady I saw did it. Black with white around it. Made a showy thing, but I wouldn't have wanted it.

But you know, I think that people weren't even as much morbid then as they are now. They just had a different way . . . as a matter of fact, you didn't hear of one-tenth the suicides then as you hear now. As a child I don't remember that I actually knew of a suicide, with the exception of one man who was mentally unbalanced and shot his wife and children and himself. *That* happened. And this Parrott boy who jumped in the water, but I was grown when I heard of that and moved here into the Lone Pine community. That did happen about nineteen and one, but that was so rare they made a ballad out of it. So very rare. And it was a mystery always why this boy killed himself.

THE DROWNDED BOY

'Twas early in the springtime, all in the month of May
A young man in deep sorrow, from home he went away.
He left his aged parents and friends to mourn his loss,
And broken-hearted parents to bear a heavy cross.

He went down to the river and stood upon the shore;
He thought of home and mother in happy days of yore.
With no mother there to guide him or father's hand to save,
He jumped into the water and sank beneath the waves.

He sank beneath the waves, no father there to save.
No mother there to guide him, he filled a watery grave.
We found him in the evening, the sun was bending low.
He'd risen on the waters and floated to the shore.
They put him in his coffin, hauled him to his grave,
And laid him there to rest and await the Judgment Day.

That song was written by the Reverend George Poole about this boy, Rufus Parrott. This happened right here in this community. He had gone to Devil's Fork to drown himself and no one has ever known why, though, of course, you hear lots of different stories. The Parrotts lived right over across the way, about a mile from here. Rev. George Poole lived there near where it happened. Parrott was buried over at Pleasant Ridge, and his funeral was preached there one year from the day he drownded. Preacher Poole preached the funeral and sang the ballad he had composed. He had written it a few days before. He and his choir sang it at that church. This song is an exception around here—

for funerals. I don't believe I've ever heard one sung like this, so you can see how unusual a suicide was around here in those days.

But you see, when we pieced quilts and sang, or we made soap, or the men worked in the fields, we kept busy. And we were well adjusted and happy. Everyone was happy in their role as wife and mother and so on. And the church and school was just about the only social gathering that we had. And I think these things meant more to us than they do today.

We couldn't worry about ourselves, the way some kids seem to do today. We were just a little too busy. Like when I was a child we quilted, and crocheted, and knitted, and plowed—I'll bet if you gave me a plow and mule I could still plow as straight a furrow as you want. As a child we knitted our own hose—stockings for girls and socks for boys. I've knitted and worn the stockings that I had knitted. I still knit gloves now and then, and if I'd do it, my boys would still wear the socks I knit.

And, too, we carded and spun. My father kept some sheep when I was a child. And this wool was shorn . . . up until I was ten years old (and many people did as late as that, back in here, this deep in Cleburne). They had their sheep, they would shear this wool off, and then you oiled it and first thing you did, you picked the burrs out of it. If there's a cocklebur any place, the sheep'll find it. And you picked that out and you put kerosene on this wool. Now you could wash it before you carded it, but it was best not to clean it, because it had this natural oil in it. You see it would help you when you carded it. Well, we carded it and we spun it. These old hand-cards had teeth in them. Like combing . . . you pulled the wool apart and combed it. And you rolled that up into little rolls and then put it on this wheel, an old spinning wheel. My mother had a spinning wheel, everybody had a spinning wheel. That wasn't a luxury, it was a necessity. And we'd spin wool thread. You'd spin two strands and then double it together and twist it—crossed your hand when you'd go to twist it. And I twisted it together—and you knit with that. Crocheted shawls, knit socks.

To color it, you could take the hulls of a walnut and set it with coprous [copperas] or alum—turned it brown, a beautiful brown. The bark of a sumac would turn it black. And the bark of hickory you dyed a beautiful yellow—that was before the Putnam dyes. Boil this, strain it out, and set it with alum after they boiled. I've dyed quilt linings with it, and it stays almost fast. And you could buy indigo. I remember Aunt Fanny Barber buying indigo and dying with that.

And you could spin and dye cotton the same way. I could spin cotton finer than I could wool—for crocheting—most people would rather spin wool, but I'd rather spin cotton. We grew the cotton but we didn't pick the seeds out. When they hauled the cotton to the gin, there was always a bagful taken out for quilting cotton and spinning cotton and things like that. Brought back home. And if the old man was too stingy about it, didn't take any out of the bale, after the cotton was picked, we'd get out and pick this scrap cotton, the ginner could gin it for the seed, and we would send all the bags down there that we wanted to.

A lot of my ballads, unfortunately, I don't know where they came from 'cause I've always had this interest in ballads. And my father encouraged it up to a point. Until, as I told you, I was about twelve or thirteen years old and was taking more interest in ballads than anything else. I think maybe if I'd a-been allowed to just keep digging, I might have gotten it out of my system. Of course, "folklore," the word was not even known then. Nobody knew anything about that, which probably was a very happy situation. I think so, because maybe if we didn't try to go so deeply, I think maybe we might enjoy what we have more. We're becoming entirely too technical in this thing. We're trying to pick it apart. I really believe that. And I think that folksongs are meant more or less like children: you're not meant to try to understand them or analyze them, just to enjoy them.

Maybe it's because we're trying to commercialize them too much. So many of us—maybe not me because I don't care much what people think . . . I guess I'm a nonconformist that way—so many people want to sing what they think people want to hear. I couldn't care less. If someone wants to hear what I'm singing, that's the one I want to sing it to. To be popular, . . . I don't care if I am or not. Some people ask me how I can sing before the congregations I do, without any embarrassment. If they didn't want to hear this in my style of singing, then why come? Then tomorrow they don't have to come back.

So, I never try to pick these songs apart, or understand them too much, just as I don't with children. I get along well with children, and I get along well with folksongs . . . by not picking them apart too much.

When you get technical, you just get too much controversy over these things. Like this "Four Marys" song. Russia's claiming it now, I read. They say that Mary Hamilton was a Russian girl. But this story, actually, I've been told by an old Scottish couple I know; they said that they had visited this place and that definitely she was an English girl come to Scotland. She was in waiting at the court of Queen Mary—Mary Stuart—Queen of Scots in the sixteenth century. But anyway, she was in waiting

FOUR MARYS

to Mary, Queen of Scots, and she became pregnant by the king's son. And she would have been beheaded for that, whether or not she killed the child, because it would have been declared illegitimate. She would have been beheaded because she had borne him for the king's son. I love "Four Marys" just the way it is. It's a beautiful ballad. And I think we could become too technical with too many stories and too much controversy.

Now, I don't know anybody that's worse about this than I am . . . that'll dig deeper and try to find out more about an old ballad than I will. I'm one of the most technical people that I know. I try to dig up everything about a story that I can. I've spent years trying to find out about "The Wife of Usher's Well," what we call "Little Lady Gay," and "Lady Margaret," and "The Four Marys," and songs like that. But I don't know if that adds to our satisfaction or not about the song. It does something for our *curiosity,* but not our satisfaction. And when we forget about the song and the satisfaction in getting too technical, then we've lost something. I think as a child I enjoyed them more when I just sang them as ballads. Took them at their worth. Didn't know they had a story behind them.

FOUR MARYS

Last night there were four Marys,
Tonight there'll only be three;
Mary Eaton, Mary Seaton,
Mary Carmichael and me.

Now word is in the kitchen
And word is out in the hall;
That Mary Hamilton goes with child
To the highest Stuart of all.

He courted her in the kitchen,
He courted her in the hall;
When he courted her down in the low cellar
That was the worst of all.

"Last night I washed my queen's feet,
Put gold braid all in her hair;
But the only thing it ever will bring to me
Is a death so sad."

Mary Hamilton goes a-weeping
Down by the deep blue sea;
"I'll bear this Stuart child alone,
And it will be the death o' me."

And the wee barn, he was stillborn,
She cast him into the sea;
"Lie there, lie there, ye king's grandson,
And you'll ha' no more need o' me."

Now down hath come the old queen,
The gold braids still in her hair;
"Mary Hamilton, where is the child
That I heard cry so sore?"

"There ne'er hath been a wee barn here
As anyone here can see;
'Twas only a touch o' my sore side
And the weeping ye heard was me."

"Now put on your dress of red, my dear,
Or either the black or brown;
For before tomorrow's sun shall set
I'll ride ye through Edinboro town."

She neither put on her dress of red
Nor yet the black or brown;
She dressed herself in pure white robes,
Yet they rode her through Edinboro town.

"Oh, little did me mother think
That day she was cradling o' me
The distant lands that I would roam
And the death I'd have to die."

"Last night there were four Marys,
Tonight there'll only be three;
Mary Eaton, Mary Seaton,
Mary Carmichael and me."

The first that brought the "Four Marys" back to my memory
was hearing it sung [by the editor] out at Idyllwild.* Before it
was finished I'd remembered a part of it, so I knew that I'd
known it before. This part about "Last night I washed my
queen's feet/Put the gold braids in her hair," that was done as

*The Idyllwild Arts Foundation, Idyllwild, California, at which Granny and I served
as faculty for two weeks in June, 1964, and where this book was dreamed up. (Ed.)

I do. And "Last night there were four Marys,/ Tonight there'll only be three." I remembered that. But as it was sung it left an unsatisfactory feeling. . . . I didn't know it as that. And Joan Baez, I heard her singing it and I didn't know that ending. So, it took me actually some months when I came home . . . I kept thinking of this, and thought of these verses here about "Mary Hamilton goes a-weeping down by the deep blue sea." Those verses I even remembered at Idyllwild. I just went on and kept those verses in my head. And when I came home, in this trunk I was cleaning up to give my sister, I kept a few things out of it. I found, on a tablet, this song. The first part was torn out and it began about there. And so I knew somewhere in my childhood, as this was written by my sister who's now buried in California, somewhere she had collected it or I had collected it and we had sung it together. I remember then singing it off and on when we were young. And I thought my Aunt Belle sang it, so as she was now passed away, I went to Pangburn, the town where I was raised mostly, and asked my double-cousins, Jack and Otis James, about it, but they didn't remember it at all. So it went for a period of a year and a half or two years. And last spring I was coming home from Tennessee and stopped off at Pangburn and visited this old friend, Grandma Gray. I sang the song to her up to this verse. I said "Now, Grandma, I've forgotten it. Can you finish it?" Yes, she knew the "Four Marys," she said. Then she sang it just as I sing it. And there was one verse toward the last that I had forgotten and didn't get together:

> When she walked to Edinb'ro town
> The heel came off'n her shoe.
> And in the court of Edinburgh
> She was condemned to die.

And here's the way she sang the last verse:

> "Last night there were four Marys,
> Tonight there'll only be three;
> Mary Eaton and Mary Beaton.
> Queen Mary's beheadin' o' me."

And that wound it up for Grandma Gray.

I told her that there was only one other person I ever heard, an old man from Tennessee, who ever sang the song that way, with the babe being stillborn, and she said, "Well, then, he must have been of Black Irish descent if he sang it like that." She said, "My grandmother and grandfather were what they called 'Black Irish.' They came from the mountains of Ireland—between Ireland and Scotland—and I learned it from my grandmother." Grandmother Gray is now about eighty-eight or eighty-nine.

Now, my grandfather said that he was Black Irish. He had dark eyes and dark hair and dark skin. They were small people. So I could have heard this from my own family. But I asked Grandma Gray where I had learned it, and she said, "From me, I guess, when you were five or six years old." She thought she remembered it, either me or my sister.

I think possibly this little sister that died, Claudy, I think possibly she and I sang it then, because we *did* sing together . . . a lot. She would teach me what she would learn, and vice versa. As I was not very old then, things are foggy. But I think maybe when she died, I just stopped singing that song, because it reminded me of her . . . the shock of Claudy's dying. I think I didn't sing for a long period . . . they tell me that actually it was a few months that I wouldn't sing at all. I just couldn't sing without Claudy. I had slept with her. I didn't even feel I could sleep without Claudy. And, incidentally, I remember that's the first that I tried to pray. I think I blocked off that song—you can do things like that. We moved across the river, then, to a place they call Big Creek; my father got a job hacking ties and I went off with him. And I was myself again and began singing. Now "Four Marys" may not be the song we were learning, but I never remembered it until Idyllwild and that brought the memory back. After I came back home, I found it was common among many people over in Pangburn. I don't know . . . I don't hear it in this area—just over there where I lived when I was a child.

Now, this "Lady Margaret" that Irene Saletan [another member of the faculty] reminded me about at Idyllwild, that's different. I remembered I had known it, and *well*, but I had to listen to her version, and that helped me to piece my version together. Then I came back and talked with Aunt Ollie Gilbert at the

Newport Festival (we roomed together there—she's an old friend of mine) and we talked about "Lady Margaret." And we sing it, Aunt Ollie and I, similar . . . not quite alike. Mine's not quite like Aunt Ollie's and it's not quite like Irene's but where they went along with it as I remembered it, I sing it as they did, and many other places I didn't . . . I just remembered it.

I don't know where I first heard it. It's a very old ballad through this area. Practically everyone knows "Lady Margaret" or a version of it, because Governor Faubus, when he dedicated our boat docks here in 1966, had asked for me to sing it. He

LADY MARGARET AND LORD WILLIAM

said that was *just* as his grandmother sang it. And Orville Faubus
is just about as old as I am. He said it there that day. He thanked
me and said to the people there that his grandmother rocked him
to sleep with that ballad. So I know it's the old version that I do.
I just used Irene's version to refresh my memory the way I would
with Lora Garrett or with any other of my neighbors around
here that help me piece together songs. It is almost, if not quite
exactly, as I heard it fifty, or perhaps sixty, years ago.

"Now what will you do, Lady Margaret?" he cried,
And "What can we do?" said she.
"For before tomorrow's sun goes down
Lord William's bride you shall see;
Lord William's bride you will see."

Lady Margaret sat in her high hall window.
Combing of her yellow hair.
When along came William from the church near by
Leading his bride so fair;
Leading his bride so fair.

She threw down that ivory comb.
Back she tossed her hair;
Down she fell to the high hall window
And never more was seen there.
Never more to go there.

Now when day was done and night come on,
The people all asleep,
Lady Margaret arose from her coffin cold,
Stood weeping at William's bed feet,
Just weeping at his bed feet.

And it's "How do you like your bed making,"
And it's "How do you like your sheet,"
And "How do you like your new-made bride
There in your arms asleep,
Lying there looking so sweet?"

Oh, it's "Well do I like my bed making,"
And it's "Well do I like my sheet.
But better would I like my old true love
Were she in my arms asleep,
Not weeping at my bed feet."

"What a dream, what a dream, what an awful dream," he said.
"I fear it means no good.
I dreamed my room was filled with tears,
My bride all drowned in blood;
My new bride drowned in blood."

He called down all his waiting men
By one, by two, and three.
"Go ask me leave of my new-made bride,
Lady Margaret I must see;
Lady Margaret I would see."

"Oh, if you go back to Lady Margaret
What will become of me?"
"Well, I won't be gone but an hour or two,
Then I'll come back to thee;
And I'll be true to thee."

And "Is she in her bowery room
Or is she in her hall,
Or is she in her chamber
A lady among them all,
Lady Margaret is fairest of all."

"No, she's not in her bowery room
And she's not in her hall.
Lady Margaret lies in a coffin cold
Out there in the hall,
With her face turned to the wall."

"Take off, take off that coffin lid,
Turn down that shroud so fine;
And let me kiss Lady Margaret's lips,
In life she oft kissed mine;
So often has kissed mine."

Her father took off the coffin lid,
Her brother turned down the sheet;
Three times he kissed her death cold lips,
Fell dead right at her feet;
Fell dead right at her feet.

Lady Margaret was buried in the old church yard.
Lord William was buried a-nigh her.
From Margaret's heart grew a red, red rose,
From William's heart a green brier;
From William's heart grew a brier.

They grew and grew to the top of the wall
'Til they couldn't grow any higher.
They looped and tied in a lover's knot
And the rose still clung to the brier;
And the rose embraced the brier.

Now this story, supposedly, you know, with some older people that you'll find, they say that she also was a commoner and lady-in-waiting with the queen. Lord William was the queen's son and that she was pregnant and committed suicide because when he married he had to take another woman. Another wife, you see, from the royal blood. But now that's all supposition. We don't know. I never found anything like that in the collections.

Just as this "face to the wall." Many of these old ballads have "They turned their face to the wall" and either died or were already dead. Well then, if they had been betrayed in love, their face was turned to the wall. If not, they weren't betrayed. Another supposition like this was that if any of the royal blood touched a corpse, they died. That was death. And Lord William knew that would mean his death when he touched her. That's an English superstition.

Like I say, when I want to learn a song, I just can't do anything else. The thing is I can't turn it off. It will stay with me and if I hear it as much as three times or if I can get a tape on it and play the tape three times, I know it—because I won't think of anything else. And before tapes, well, I would just get a ballet on it, and if I wanted the tune I'd note it at the top of the ballet, then I'd have it. There'll be three or four days or a week or possibly longer where that song or nothing else will run through my mind. I'll sing it constantly. And though I may forget what people tell me or I may forget where I put the dishrag, my thimbles, my needles (I'm always losing things), but I never forget a song. I may forget it for awhile but when somebody will sing a word or two of it, it'll come back.

Sometimes though, like with "Barbara Allen" and those that everyone sings, I'll mix up versions once in awhile. I'll tell you the story on a song I dearly love—"The Merry Golden Tree" — because it's gotten so complicated in my mind. It was all on this ship, she was spotted by the *Spanish Robberie,* and the little

boy sank the robbers, and then the captain sailed off and left
them too. Well, one of the first times I heard it was from this
friend of my husband and I, Brother Donohue. He was an Irishman and he could give you that Irish twang. But he sang it that
when she sailed off and left the little boy, sure enough in a week,
from two to three, she was spotted by *another* ship, British, and
sunk.

> Then she sailed around
> A week from two to three,
> And there she spotted the *British Robberie*.
> They were sailing on that high, low,
> Lonesome high, low,
> Lonesome lowland sea.
>
> The ship sailed by jumps
> And she sailed by spurts,
> But the Jolly Roger gave her
> Her just desserts,
> For they sank her in the high, low,
> Lonesome high, low,
> Lonesome lowland sea.

Brother Donohue was a Baptist minister and a full-blooded
Irishman. And one of the finest men I've ever known. He lived
back over here on the mountain. I became acquainted with him
after I became a mother. We were close friends, he and his wife
and us. He was as old as my father, and their children were
grown. He sang that song one night when we were there. Elder
Russell and I and my husband were there. I think we were mov-
ing away from there and we had taken this loaded wagon up
there to spend the night. Elder Russell or I or somebody sug-
gested that we sing some songs. Brother Donohue said, "I'll sing
you one. I'll sing you 'The Golden Willow Tree.' " And he sang
that version of "The Golden Vanity."

Then we came on down here and moved into this vicinity. In
the meantime, my sister Verdie was singing "The Merry Golden
Tree," which she had learned from her mother-in-law. So she
sang me this one, and I learned this version. Later I forgot some
of these verses, so I wrote and had Aunt Mabel Starks, her mother-
in-law, send them to me.

THE GOLDEN WILLOW TREE

There was a little ship that sailed upon the sea,
And the name of that ship was the *Golden Willow Tree,*
Sailing on the low and lonesome low,
Sailing on the lonesome sea.

Now she hadn't been out but a week, two or three,
Until she sighted the *British Robberie,*
Sailing on the low and lonesome low,
Flaunting the Jolly Roger on the lowland sea.

Up stepped the captain, wringing of his hands,
Saying, "Alas, what shall we do?
They will sink us in this low and lonesome low,
They will sink us in this lonely lowland sea."

A boy then said, "Captain, what will you give me
If I sink this *British Robberie?*
I'll sink them in this low and lonesome low,
I'll sink them to the bottom of this lonely sea."

"I'll give you wealth, I'll give you fee,
My oldest daughter and you shall married be,
If you'll sink them in this low and lonely low,
If you'll sink them in this lonely sea."

Then he picked up a tool and he jumped overboard.
He said, "I'll be as good as my word."
And he was swimming in the low and lonesome low,
Swimming in the lonesome, lowland sea.

Then he took his little tool, just made for that use,
And he made twelve holes just to let in the juice,
And she was sinking in the low and lonesome low,
She was sinking in the lonesome lowland sea.

The sailors offed with their coats and same with their caps,
All trying to fill up the salt water gaps,
But they sunk in the low and lonesome low,
They sank to the bottom of the lonesome sea.

Then he turned around and away swam he
Till he came back to the *Golden Willow Tree.*
Swimming in the low and lonely low,
Still swimming in the lonely lowland sea.

"Oh, captain, are you good as your word?
Then take this poor sailor man aboard.
For I'm drowning in this low and lonesome low,
I'm drowning in this lonely lowland sea."

"I will not give you wealth, nor give you your fee,
Nor my oldest daughter to you shall married be.
I'll just leave you in this low and lonesome low,
I'll just leave you in this lonesome lowland sea."

"Well, if it wasn't for your daughter and your being such a man,
I would do unto you what I did to them.
I'd sink you in this low and lonesome low,
I'd sink you to the bottom of this lonesome sea."

Then he turned on his back and away floated he,
Saying, "Fare you well, *Golden Willow Tree,*
I'm drowning in this low and lonesome low,
I'm drowning in this lonely lowland sea."

Aunt Mabel told me she learned it from her mother or her
grandmother. She had sung it one night—Verdie said that they
were fixing beds. They'd all gone to her mother-in-law's house to

spend the night and she was fixing the bed and singing this song. My sister had her to write it for her and she then taught it to me—just memorized it and sang it—never had time to write it, with plowing and hoeing and nursing of a night to do. Then after Verdie moved away and died, then I had time to write out my songs, so I began to reconstruct this thing. When I went to write it out, though, I had it confused with "The Golden Willow Tree" of Brother Donohue's, and this I found out when I got Aunt Mabel's ballet. But I've been doing it that way for twenty-five years, so there's no reason to bother with it now. It's her tune, and it's mostly her version.

Mabel did it this way, for instance:

> He took his little tool
> Just made for that use,
> And he bored twelve holes
> And he let in the juice.

I don't think I usually do it that way. And here was Brother Donohue's version:

> From his box of tools,
> He took a little bit,
> And he bored twelve holes
> In the bottom of the ship.

Now this is Aunt Mabel's here, and Brother Donohue didn't have this in his:

> The sailors off with their coats,
> Some took off their caps,
> All trying for to fill up
> Those salt water gaps.
> Yet they sank her in the lowland, lonesome low.
> And she sank to the bottom of the lowland sea.

I think this is much the prettier ballad, really, nice as Brother Donohue's is.

After Brother Donohue was old, he spent a night here and I asked him about this "High, low, lonesome, low." I sang Aunt

Mabel's version and he said, "That don't go like that." But he had forgotten a lot of it by that time. It had been over twenty years, and he was in his eighties by then. And so I never got that other beautiful version completely, and I don't know that *anyone* knows it.

The only actual difference is in the endings. I don't know why I didn't put in those last verses, because they're nice ones. I guess I just don't like to consciously doctor a song, a traditional song. If it had been of my own making, that would be different—would have made a good one. I've known that to be done. I believe that in the original that did go in, because it does make a complete ending. She first sighted the *Spanish Robberie* and then the *British Robberie*. But I've never seen it in any collection. He got his just desserts in that one ballet, so somebody might have made that verse up. I'd just as soon be accused of writing a hot check than to change a ballad like that.

So that's all there is about my songs and myself. And as far as I'm concerned, that's a good deal too much about me—and maybe not enough about the songs. But I'll tell you one thing: I've sung ever since I remember. I intend to sing as long as God gives me a cracked-up voice to do it with. And I intend to sing these songs. But my one greatest, pushing ambition is to get all of the songs I know either on tape or in book form and leave it. Free for anybody that wants to use it. And you can sign that: Granny Riddle.

Afterword

There are certain features of this book that I, as a folklorist, want to point up. This is something of a unique book in Anglo-American folksong scholarship in that its focus is on a performer rather than on texts. There have been other works which have presented the repertoires of performers having equally large lists. Virtually every major regional collection relies upon tradition-bearers of this sort. We have occasionally had works which presented the repertoire of one performer—books like those of Jean Ritchie, or such as Jean Thomas' *Singing Fiddler of Lost Hope Hollow,* (New York, 1938). The books by L. L. and Flora McDowell, *Memory Melodies* (Smithville, Tenn., 1947) and *Songs of the Old Camp Ground* (Ann Arbor, Mich., 1937) record their repertoire, as probably do Fred High's *Old, Old Folksongs* (Berryville, Ark. n.d.), M. C. Dean's *The Flying Cloud* (Quickpoint, Minn., 1922) and *A Pioneer Songster* (Ithaca, N.Y., 1958), edited by Harold S. Thompson and Edith C. Cutting. Edward D. Ives has studied the songs composed by one traditional song-maker in his *Larry Gorman, the Man Who Made the Songs* (Bloomington, Ind., 1964). However, only the study by Leonard Roberts of the Couch family traditions, *Up Cutshin and Down Greasy* (Lexington, Ky., 1959) has focused, as this volume does, on the ways in which folklore has persisted, emphasizing the hows and whys of performance and transmission.

Such studies are important merely because they bring the

performer into the foreground, thereby rectifying in part the tendency to divorce the singer from the songs, the teller from the tales. But this change of focus has important by-products. Through it we understand a great deal more about the process of transmission. For instance, if one reads the folksong literature only to understand how songs reside in the memories of performers, one would be totally ignorant of the fact that each song almost always has some kind of legend associated with it which enhances its emotional impact. Such legends may be *memorat*; that is, they may relate to how the song was originally learned, from whom, and under what circumstances. The singer commonly associates a song with a specific singer and this therefore assists in the memory process. Other song legends may refer to the supposed events behind the song; in these cases, understanding of the "emotional core" of the song is incomplete without the accompanying details. Furthermore, this kind of legend may account in part for changes which occur in a song; elements may be dropped or added from this fund of narrative traits and motives. We see, for instance, just such a process working in Granny's explanation of "Little Lady Gay," for, though she has lost the verses concerning the wetting of the winding sheet, that element still remains part of the story because of the accompanying legend.

It is because of the importance of these details in an understanding of the traditional process, and not merely because of a desire to make the study more "folky," that it has seemed important to make this book into a "folk-autobiography." But my desires in this regard were not shared by Granny, who repeatedly asked why anybody would want to hear so much about *her* when the songs were so much more important. It was only through extended explanation that I was able to convince her that these matters were important in an understanding of the kind of person who is attracted to these songs and who therefore both has kept the tradition alive and has been a folk artist within the small community. In this I stressed to her that I was not concerned as much with the details of her life as the way in which she represents the way in which good singers function (or used to function) in rural American communities.

One of the problems facing the social scientist today (and I include myself in that group, if a bit hesitantly) is establishing a balance between the larger patterns of a culture and the individuals in it who subscribe in whole or in part to those habits of action and thought which exhibit the style of the culture being investigated. There has been a significant literature in the last generation which has utilized a "life history" approach to culture and society, works which analyze a group through the lives and talk of a few representative individuals. Such a technique has been especially evident in those interested in "Culture and Personality." More recently, this approach has been presented to a wide general public in the works of Oscar Lewis, the most recent being *La Vida*. But whereas those of the Culture and Personality School have tended to bury the interviewed individuals in the machinery of their analysis, Lewis has eschewed the use of such paraphernalia, apparently feeling that the words of his informants say everything about the situation being explored that needs to be said; but, as many critics point out, we don't know when the informant's voice ends and the editorial hand begins, a problem especially critical in translated materials.

The folklorist has worked as closely with informants as has the anthropologist, and he has been even more involved in setting down the actual words of the informant. Yet the folklorist, in most cases, has not much cared about these words except as they achieved some kind of naive art and echoed the aesthetic principles and preoccupations of the past. The implicit view seems to have been that traditional art exists apart from performance; the singer has simply provided a convenient voice through which these relics, these anachronisms could find one last-gasping performance. I hope that this work will exorcise that idea, as well as any persistence of the notions that the folk have no aesthetic, or no collectors of their own, or no individuals worthy of study as individuals.

In a sense, folklorists have arrived at their point of view as an embellishment of a very real attitude on the part of the Anglo-American traditional performer that singers *are* only mouthpieces for songs descended to them. This is the essence of Granny's distinction between "performing" and "presenting."

But I think her elaborations of the song-learning process show that the scholar's extension of this performance attitude into a critical precept is somewhat misguided. To view a singer like Granny as a simple "tradition-bearer" is to reduce her role in the traditional process to only one of its significant facets. She *is* a "traditor," to be sure, but she has also asserted her individuality in a number of ways that are important for students of culture to note. She is not only a singer, but also a lifelong collector of ballads and a writer and rewriter of songs—in fact, a person who has virtually lived her life in songs and whose values are reflected in the choice of the songs she will sing.

These songs have been preserved because certain tradition-oriented individuals and communities have found them of value in their lives. It therefore seems important to investigate the life and values of someone who has emerged from a traditional background, found importance in these songs as a way of giving order to her life, yet who seems to cling to these older ways with greater fervor than most other members of her communiy.

In fact, Granny is regarded, as she puts it, as something of a "kook" in her neighborhood. They don't think of her as the best singer. That position is reserved for the men with big voices, such as her father and Uncle Bob Starks had, and Granny holds the same view of her place in the singing community.

It is instructive to visit with Granny to see how her song-hunting and recent travels are regarded. Many neighbors seem to think that her search for ballads is a mild nuisance, seeming to say that "the old girl never grew up." Nonetheless, a good number of them share her love for the old ways and will help her out however they can.

When a song which she used to know begins to come back to her—this most often happens when she is away doing concerts and thus hears more songs than usual—she can't rest until she can piece the song together exactly as she used to sing it. This means that she will get on the phone with one of her singer friends, most often her neighbor Lora Garrett, and say, "Remember that piece about . . .? Let me sing you a snatch that just came to me. Can you remember how we used to sing that?" These conversations may go on for an hour. If the phone fails her, she is liable to flag down a truck passing along her road because she sees someone driving it with whom she went to school and he may remember the song. If the song still is not complete, and it often is not, she will get someone to drive her to Pangburn or to Heber Springs to visit other singers or relatives. The single-mindedness of her oral researching would put most scholars to shame, although she has none of the patience or objectivity of the social scientist. "Badgering" and "wheedling" are the words that keep coming to mind in regard to her elicitation of songs. Any new song will interest her, but only a song she used to sing will truly excite her.

If she does not have the scholar's objectivity, she does have a full measure of his fervor for authenticity. This has led her to attempt to remember where and from whom she learned a song. She wants to recall her own versions of songs because she can know from her own experience that these are authentic. This fervor has also led her to look at any old songbook she can get her hands on, not only as a source of songs but as reassurance that the songs she sings are old and authentic folksongs.

She has not had this feeling instilled in her by folklorists, I am reasonably sure, although such contacts have certainly both intensified this attitude and brought it out into a conscious expression of her values. One doubts whether she would ever have made the distinction between *presenting* and *performing,* for instance, had she not been at a number of folk festivals in recent years with scholars like John Quincy Wolf, A. L. Lloyd, D. K. Wilgus, Charles Seeger, and Kenneth Goldstein and sat with them in panel discussions which were directly concerned with matters of style, tradition, and authenticity.

Through experiences of this sort, she has become very conscious of the criteria used by scholars to determine validity. This affected the repertoire included in the book, though how deeply it is difficult to say. Her distinction between classic and nonclassic songs seems to affect her present choice of favorites, and it may not be simply by chance that most of those which she terms classic are Child ballads. On the other hand, some of them are not;

and she may be equating age with dignity in giving one the name of "classic," for they often are songs whose tradition in her family she can trace.

Her consciousness of scholarly precepts came out forcefully with one song-ballet which she had in her collection—"Peggy of Glasgow." I told her that this ballad would excite certain scholars very much because it had never been reported in the New World. Her reply was, "Well, that one *won't* go in the book." Her reasons were that she didn't want anyone to impugn the authenticity of her songs; one bad apple might spoil the barrel. She could not remember from whom she got the song, and the tune eluded her consistently. Even though I showed her from internal evidence that the song must have come from an authentic oral source (see my notes) this did not alter her mind in regard to even recording the song for my own records.

On the other hand, the uniqueness of her "Mary Hamilton" or her "Rare Willie Drowned in Yarrow" texts did not worry her in the least (although the latter is remarkably close to that in Leach's *Ballad Book*) because she had a complete remembrance of having sung the songs in childhood and she was able to have this verified by other members of her community (verification which I corroborated in both instances).

So we can, by no stretch of the imagination, view Granny as the "ideal" folk informant since she knows so much about her own songs and her tradition. This is clear from the bookish words she uses in describing her songs and her tradition and from the argot she uses, picked up from folkniks while on the festival trail. Furthermore, unlike the ideal informant, rather than thinking that her versions are the only true ones, she knows that even in her own community one song may be sung in many different ways. This does not mean that she won't argue over which is the authentic *family* version. We know she will from her description of the Frog and Mouse song (that discussion was much cut for the sake of readability here).

On the other hand, she is the ideal informant in the sense that she knows her repertoire very well—it is limitless (the songs here are probably just a surface scratch, although they are the ones she values most highly just now)—and she sings only what she considers to be complete versions of her songs. In fact, it is almost impossible to get her to sing a song fragment unless she happens to be searching for the rest of the words at that time.

Matters of this sort point to the fund of information which Granny has given on the subject of the role the individual may play while remaining a tradition-bearer. During our many discussion sessions a good deal of information has surfaced which has direct bearing on the whole question of performer and audience attitudes that permits us to see in somewhat clearer perspective some of the ramifications of tradition-oriented approach. Perhaps of greatest importance to Granny in her approach to a specific song is whether it is a "classic" or not. Classic songs are those she considers to be the oldest (and do indeed include all of the Child ballads in her repertoire, plus a number of the broadside, and some of her sentimental ballads.) Clearly this has been a distinction which has operated on her attitudes and her performances all of her singing life. And the importance of the distinction is that classic songs may not be changed, in theory, while others can be by whoever cares to. The most extensive group of songs that may be altered is children's songs (other than the immutable "Frog and Mouse"), which indicates that the distinction may arise as much from a perceived performer-audience difference than actual age. This comes in her discussion of her unusual version of the children's "Go Tell Aunt Nancy," which she recognizes as a very old song but one which she "never sings the same way twice."

This important contextual feature distinguishing between different approaches to adult and child audiences is further under-lined and amplified in her pronouncements on singing technique. She insists that a good traditional singer must *present* and not *perform* the songs. By this she means that the song must come first, that the singer must not throw himself into the singing. But she does point out that she often has to *perform* if she is singing to children.

Parallel to this distinction in performance attitudes is a deep sense of a need for *appropriateness* of songs. For Granny the really important distinctions are the ones arising from a determination of who makes up the audience, and once again the central distinction is between children and adults. There are certain songs which Granny sees as appropriate to children's groups that are somewhat nonsensical to sing to adults, and she is uncomfortable doing so. This has come out in a number of ways in our conversations, the most common being that she has been asked consistently by adults at concerts and folk festivals to sing certain songs which she considers appropriate to children, a situation she has humorously rationalized in terms of "the child" in everyone—but she remains uncomfortable in singing the songs and complains in private about repeatedly being forced to sing "China Doll" or" Go Tell Aunt Nancy" to such audiences. This situation is paralleled by her feeling that certain sad or bloody songs are inappropriate for children, but she recognizes that these are often the very songs that children, even in her own family, want most to hear.

This sense of appropriateness appears perhaps even more clearly in her reluctance to sing certain songs before *any* audience. There are a number of songs which she knows but does not like to sing, and others which she has heard but will not learn, even while recognizing that the song is a "classic" (such is the case, for instance, with "Little Mattie Groves.") Obscene songs are, of course, simply not a part of her repertoire, though she admits to enjoying hearing them occasionally, if they are sung by a woman in a small group of other females; she has a friend who has accompanied her on the folk festival circuit who, Granny notes, (without mentioning names) knows a large number of such songs. But these are not the only kinds of songs she does not sing; courting songs in dialog do not attract her—probably because she thinks them appropriate only to courting situations. And in another dimension, there are certain songs which she so strongly identifies with the singing of certain men that she considers them men's songs. In this regard, she knows "The Oxford Girl" but identifies it with the singing of her late husband and therefore does not like to sing it because "it's too bloody—it's really a man's song."

Such a discussion points to one of the most important, and most seldom investigated, areas of the role of the individual (and of individuality) in the development of repertoire—that is, what the determinants of song choice are, and what songs are learned and constantly sung, and which ones are learned but become an inactive part of the repertoire. There has been some resuscitation recently concerning the distinction between active and passive tradition-bearers. But it must also be recognized, as Kenneth S. Goldstein emphasized in a recent paper, that each song does not occupy an equal place of importance in the repertoire of an active and recognized performer. There will naturally be a wide range of songs going from those one sings all of the time (which can easily be determined through open elicitation of songs), through songs which used to be sung but have drifted into the inactive side of the repertoire, to those songs which have either been completely forgotten or which will not be sung under any circumstances because of some value criterion. With any accomplished singer like Granny, there are going to be those songs which are sung on nearly every appropriate occasion, which simply spring to mind immediately when the singing begins. And there are others which one learns about only because one continues to ask for different items from her repertoire. Sometimes the songs which come up are seldom sung simply because they are in the "back of her memory"; asking for the song may therefore bring it back into the active part of her repertoire (and this has happened many times recently, simply because she has been singing more and has been asked more questions about songs).

But some songs will be displaced because of other characteristics or accompanying associations which will block remembrance of the song. This was almost certainly the case with Granny's version of "The Three Marys," which she now knows she associated with a sister who died when she was very young, a sister to whom she was very attached and whose death brought about something of a nervous collapse on Granny's part. These negative psychological features are paralleled by certain positive forces on song choice, such as the one reported by Ellen Stekert. She noticed that, while repeatedly interviewing a male traditional singer, the same songs kept coming up in the same order at the beginning of their recording and that the content and progression of the songs bore a definite relation to their specific man-woman relationship. This situation is similar to one encountered in my first collecting experiences; I went with a collector-singer, Paul Clayton Worthington, who had a long-standing joking relationship with his aged female informant, Mrs. Marybird MacAllister, one which brought about a ritualized series of complaints on her part that he did not visit her often enough, followed by a discussion of an old man living nearby who was showing her some attentions, and then songs in which the whole idea of old-men courters was ridiculed.

But let me return for the moment to Granny's discussion of classic songs and the importance of *presenting* them rather than *performing* them. This argument is a forceful rationale for singing songs in a traditional subdued style and in the form in which the song was first learned. But this sense of traditional impersonality and removal is counteracted in part by Granny's strong predilection for singing only songs which are complete and which make sense. Because of this she usually bothers to learn only song versions which are long and tell a story completely and logically. If she likes a song very well but is dissatisfied with its sense, she does not hesitate to change it, either in phrasing or in substance, but this situation has not arisen too often, she says.

In this regard, her discussion of "The Golden Vanity" is of importance. For here she is confronted with the paradox inherent in wanting to sing a song just as she has learned it and desiring to sing as full a version as she possibly can. She sings a long and attractive version of the ballad which she learned from an old friend and relation by marriage, Mabel Starks. But before she learned it, she had heard another old friend, Brother Donohue, sing a version in which, after the cabin boy drowns, the ship which the cruel captain commands is sunk, a feature which is not found in her usual version (and which is, indeed, unique to any reporting). She likes that ending for two reasons: because there are now a balanced pair of ship-sinkings, described in similar terms, and because it accords with her feeling toward the captain and his "just desserts." She realizes that she has not added the stanzas because the version she learned did not contain them. But at the same time she recognizes that there have been other songs in which she has made similar changes in order to fill in a story or to make sense out of it. Almost certainly the reason she hasn't made such a change in this instance is because her version was complete unto itself as she learned it and therefore did not trouble her to the point she felt it demanded the added stanzas. In fact, she probably had not thought about the differences in the story until we had discussed them during our interview sessions. Thus we might say that in terms of the narrative dimension of a traditional song, to Granny, that the most important motives are fidelity and integrity on the one hand, and fullness and sense on the other.

There is a further element of individuality in the Anglo-American tradition which can be fully discerned only through comparative techniques. This involves a knowledge of the total range of the types of songs found in this culture and, therefore, an ability to see which songs and song-types have been selected by the performer. Here Granny's repertoire once again provides interesting characteristic patterns. Not only are the items important which she sings on proper occasions, or those sung seldom or never, but also those song-types to which she is attracted and those which she has not chosen to learn.

A great deal of this negative kind of information was gathered by me at the end of our taping procedures when I wanted to see how wide her passive repertoire is. To test this, I took the two largest collections from her region—Belden and Randolph—and methodically asked whether she knew each song. There were few that she said she had never heard; most brought about a reply, "Know it but don't sing it." Because both these collections are organized, in part, by song-type, she sometimes was brought to the point of giving three or four of the titles I had read recently and saying, "That's a type of song that I just have never cared to sing." The kinds of songs which got such response were, in addition to the courting dialogs, forlorn-lover lyric songs, good-time and frolic songs, songs of mockery (a couple of these local

songs she will sing and enjoy in private), ballads of sexual embarrassment, and "coon songs" (the one exception to the last being
"Kitty Wells," which does not have dialect and stereotype cues).

Illustrative of these rejections, I once asked her to tape a comic
song "Down in Arkansaw" which she had recorded for Alan
Lomax a few years before, and she could not remember the words.
But if a theme or situation conforms to her standards of interest
and beauty she will learn every song she encounters which
explores the subject. This is why she sings so many dying soldier,
cowboy, graveyard, railroad, and parted-lover ballads, shape-note
and brush-arbor songs. Her repertoire is all of a piece.

Consequently, the material given here is significant not only
for the human-interest dimension added to the songs. By investi-
gations of this sort we can begin to get a fuller understanding of
the role played by the individual in the on-going creative process
of the tradition. We are able to see that, although the tradition-
orientation toward both songs and performances remains extremely strong in such a culture, there is a variety of ways in
which an individual singer may distinguish himself. If "creativity"
exists in such a tradition, it is in the area of understanding of
and capitalizing upon community values and expectations by
individual singers, in the attitude toward the songs in terms of
artistic entities and as conveyors of sense and story, this leading
to an individual definition of repertoire. It is thus in the positive
and negative attractions toward songs and song-types, and in the
remembering and piecing together of the song versions that we
have our clearest evidence for individuality.

In surveying these factors in Granny's background and attitudes,
I may have given the impression that she lives in a tradition-
oriented community. To the contrary, there are few who share
her approach to life and her passion for the old songs. She lives
by herself in a house built in part by herself, but next door to
her daughter and near most of the rest of her family. She is
therefore surrounded by her children and grandchildren and great
grandchildren whom she warmly loves and who return her affection. But she clings to her independence and need for solitude,

something which her family seems both to admire and worry about. Some are proud enough of her doings to keep a scrapbook of concert programs and newspaper writeups, while others (those who were closest to her mother) think her travels and concerts are nonsense, and sometimes embarrassing. Thus the differences between her mother's and her father's attitudes toward "traipsing" seem to be still in evidence in other generations of her family.

Finally, it seems important to talk about the book itself from the point of view of my place in the whole proceedings. Granny's image of herself has emerged with single-minded concentration on Almeda Riddle, the singer and collector. This may reflect how she really lives her life. It may result from having an audience of folkniks and singers in mind in conceiving the book. Or it may arise from having told me, a folklorist, the details of her life, her attitudes, and her songs. The book, as it stands, is a compromise between the songbook she wanted and the life of a folk performer that I thought would be most important and interesting. The material was gathered through tape recording sessions held on three occasions, June and July, 1964, February, 1965, and April, 1967. We would talk, sometimes into the microphone, sometimes not, for about ten days each time. After each period the tapes were transcribed and I made up a list of further questions. Sometimes I saved them for further recording sessions, sometimes I wrote or phoned Granny for the answers. Meanwhile, Granny wrote a text of each song she sang for me if it was not already in her ballet book. I promised her that the book would be readable if she would let me include the material on her life and her tastes. Consequently, I have edited a great deal, while trying to keep her speech cadences in the prose. There is nothing here which Granny did not say, but the order, the syntax, and, occasionally, the grammar have been somewhat regularized. I have changed the spelling and punctuation of the songtexts to facilitate reading, but I have not changed words except to make them conform to recorded version.

I include, as appendices, annotations of the songs included in the book, a list of some of the other songs in Granny's repertoire, and finally a list of the songs in her ballet book. Reproduced copies of her songs and of the ballet book are on deposit at the Archives of the Center for Intercultural Studies in Folklore and Oral History, the University of Texas, and are available to interested persons.

ROGER D. ABRAHAMS
University of Texas

Editorial Note and Musical Analysis

The musical transcriptions of Granny Riddle's songs are intended to present the spirit if not the letter of her singing. This is because Almeda Riddle is a traditional singer—only more so. Her singing style and repertoire are deeply rooted in the Anglo-American tradition of the Ozarks but she possesses an innate musicality and sureness of performance that distinguish her from many equally authentic folksingers. This exceptional talent has gained for her a considerable success in performing for folk festivals, university concerts, and commercial recordings of folksong. Mrs. Riddle's exceptional memory, strong voice, and natural musicianship allow her to approach the presentation of a song with a relaxed confidence rare in traditional performers. Bertrand Bronson, in the introduction to volume one of his magnum opus *The Traditional Tunes of the Child Ballads*, says of traditional performers, that "the singer 'knows the tune' and thinks he is singing it all the time. Actually, he is singing variations on a musical idea." This statement is true of Granny Riddle to a degree much greater than it is of most of the informants who supplied the life of Bronson's collection. Just as superior technique and musical skills enable a jazz performer to venture further from the given musical idea in his improvisation than less gifted colleagues, the gifted traditional singer will possess the confidence to stray further from his single "musical idea." The most important difference in this comparison, however, is that the jazz artist is consciously and intentionally seeking variation as a creative means of expression while the traditional performer produces variations in an unintentional or subconscious but nonetheless creative way.

161

Almeda Riddle is extremely speech oriented in her approach to folksong, both in her attention to narrative detail and use of musical variation to fit smaller word patterns. She not only cultivates full and meaningful texts but creates a rich flexibility within the tune to accommodate the changing speech from stanza to stanza. After one listens many hours to her taped songs, it becomes apparent that she immerses herself in the language and literal meaning of her song and relies upon her strong musical sense and solid voice to keep her to the tune which she knows. Thus her musical variations are not only unselfconscious but they greatly enhance the story she has to tell or the thought she has to get across.

To transcribe fully such singing in all its detail and variety would place unrealistic demands upon the transcriber, the book designer, and certainly the reader. It would require virtually a full transcription of each verse of every song, complete with a detailed account of music, text and prosidy. This would fall far outside the scope and intent of this book and indeed would be but a single frozen example of Granny's art because at the next performance of these songs, she would undoubtedly vary her variations again.

The tunes are represented here as abstractions or the musical ideas which Granny Riddle "knows." They are first to be considered and studied apart from their words, just as one might learn to whistle or hum a tune as a pure musical idea free of any literal meaning. Once the tune is totally familiar and we truly "know it," then we use it as the framework upon which to string the words. The tunes are transcribed and arranged to show a direct relationship between the musical and verse structure with each stanza requiring a repetition of the entire tune. If the reader learns the songs in this book in this fashion, the final result will be much closer to Granny Riddle's style and spirit than could be achieved in any other way.

The meters in the transcriptions are limited to those basic musical meters which most closely relate to the folk verse of each song. The strict alternation of strong and weak pulses which is characteristic of Anglo-American folk verse is equated musically as follows: the first beat of each bar represents a strong pulse, the second beat in the bar of 2/4 and 6/8 meters represents a weak pulse, the third beat of 3/4 meter represents a weak pulse, the third beat of 4/4 meter represents a weak pulse. Therefore, each musical bar represents one strong pulse followed by its alternating weak pulse as a single unit (dipod). The variable number of unstressed syllables falling between the strong and weak pulses must be accommodated by an equally varying number of musical notes falling between the beats designated as strong and weak. This characteristic, called isochronicism, is responsible for the greatest musical variation from stanza to stanza.

The tempo of each song is indicated in metronome beats per minute before each tune.

All tunes have been transposed so as to place the final tone on the pitch g¹. This is done to provide a consistency for analysis and ease of reading and to facilitate comparison of tunes within the collection. The actual pitch levels of the recorded performances are indicated by the small catch notes which precede the analysis of each tune. The final is indicated as a white note (o) and the extremes of range are indicated as small black notes (:).

The analysis of each tune is presented in this section under the title and in the same sequence found in the book. An abstract representation of each scale is given, with all tones distributed as they appear in the tune itself. Thus, the nature and distribution of each scale are readily apparent. The numbers under each scale tone designate relative duration of that particular tone within the entire tune. The key to the duration is the small note in parentheses before each scale. For example, in the first tune, "The House Carpenter's Wife," the note has the value of an eighth note, thus the number 12 under the note "g" specifies that pitch as having a total duration during the tune equal to twelve eighth notes or six full beats. By this method the relative "importance" with regard to duration of each pitch found in the tune can be compared.

The descriptions and classifications of each scale are made in accordance with the methods outlined in *Anglo-American Folksong Style*, by Roger Abrahams and George Foss.

GEORGE FOSS
Louisiana State University

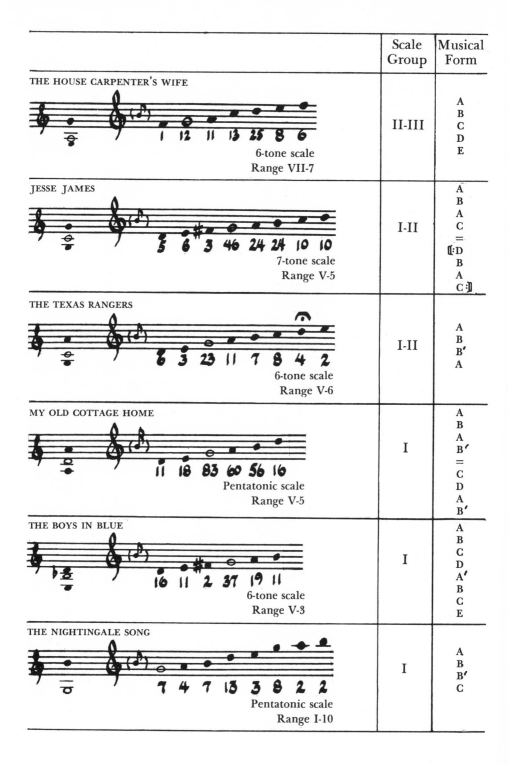

	Scale Group	Musical Form
THE HOUSE CARPENTER'S WIFE 6-tone scale Range VII-7	II-III	A B C D E
JESSE JAMES 7-tone scale Range V-5	I-II	A B A C = [:D B A C:]
THE TEXAS RANGERS 6-tone scale Range V-6	I-II	A B B' A
MY OLD COTTAGE HOME Pentatonic scale Range V-5	I	A B A B' = C D A B'
THE BOYS IN BLUE 6-tone scale Range V-3	I	A B C D A' B C E
THE NIGHTINGALE SONG Pentatonic scale Range I-10	I	A B B' C

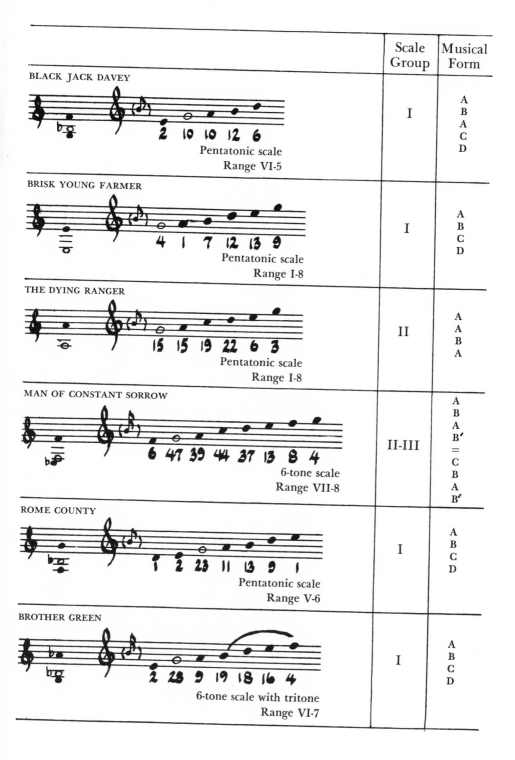

	Scale Group	Musical Form
BLACK JACK DAVEY Pentatonic scale Range VI-5 2 10 10 12 6	I	A B A C D
BRISK YOUNG FARMER Pentatonic scale Range I-8 4 1 7 12 13 9	I	A B C D
THE DYING RANGER Pentatonic scale Range I-8 15 15 19 22 6 3	II	A A B A
MAN OF CONSTANT SORROW 6-tone scale Range VII-8 6 47 39 44 37 13 8 4	II-III	A B A B′ = C B A B′
ROME COUNTY Pentatonic scale Range V-6 1 2 23 11 13 9 1	I	A B C D
BROTHER GREEN 6-tone scale with tritone Range VI-7 2 23 9 19 18 16 4	I	A B C D

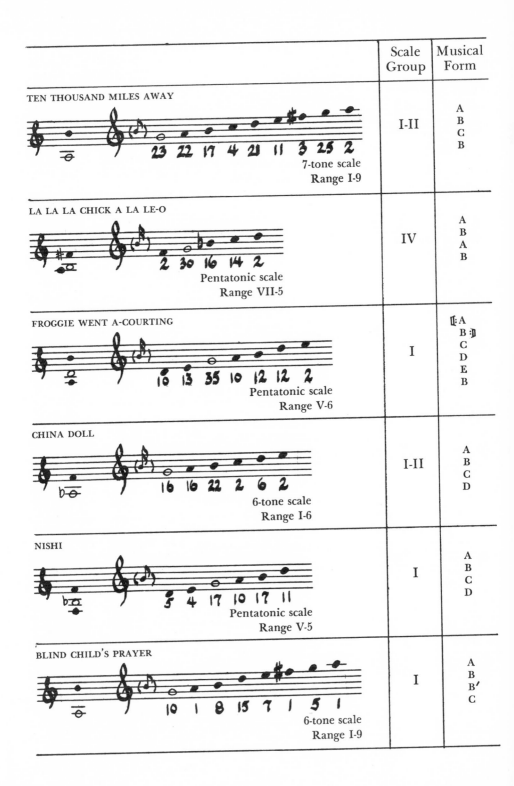

	Scale Group	Musical Form
TEN THOUSAND MILES AWAY 7-tone scale Range I-9	I-II	A B C B
LA LA LA CHICK A LA LE-O Pentatonic scale Range VII-5	IV	A B A B
FROGGIE WENT A-COURTING Pentatonic scale Range V-6	I	‖:A B:‖ C D E B
CHINA DOLL 6-tone scale Range I-6	I-II	A B C D
NISHI Pentatonic scale Range V-5	I	A B C D
BLIND CHILD'S PRAYER 6-tone scale Range I-9	I	A B B' C

166

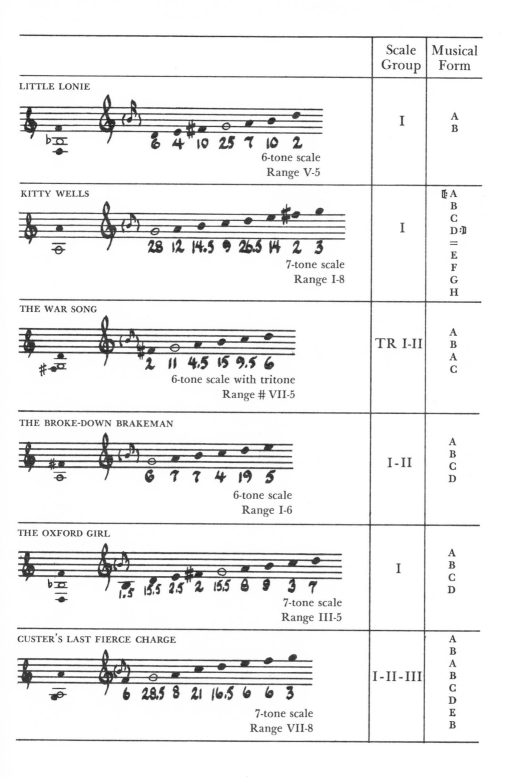

	Scale Group	Musical Form
LITTLE LONIE — 6-tone scale, Range V-5	I	A B
KITTY WELLS — 7-tone scale, Range I-8	I	A B C D·D = E F G H
THE WAR SONG — 6-tone scale with tritone, Range # VII-5	TR I-II	A B A C
THE BROKE-DOWN BRAKEMAN — 6-tone scale, Range I-6	I-II	A B C D
THE OXFORD GIRL — 7-tone scale, Range III-5	I	A B C D
CUSTER'S LAST FIERCE CHARGE — 7-tone scale, Range VII-8	I-II-III	A B A B C D E B

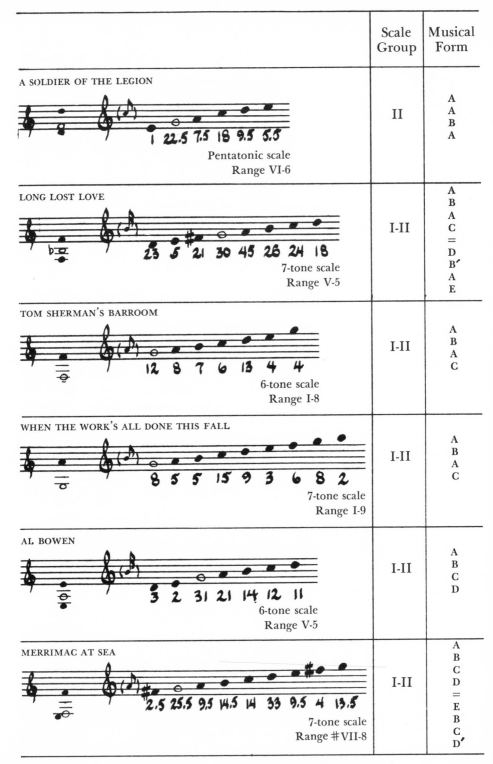

	Scale Group	Musical Form
A SOLDIER OF THE LEGION 1 22.5 7.5 18 9.5 5.5 Pentatonic scale Range VI-6	II	A A B A
LONG LOST LOVE 23 5 21 30 45 26 24 18 7-tone scale Range V-5	I-II	A B A C = D B´ A E
TOM SHERMAN'S BARROOM 12 8 7 6 13 4 4 6-tone scale Range I-8	I-II	A B A C
WHEN THE WORK'S ALL DONE THIS FALL 8 5 5 15 9 3 6 8 2 7-tone scale Range I-9	I-II	A B A C
AL BOWEN 3 2 31 21 14 12 11 6-tone scale Range V-5	I-II	A B C D
MERRIMAC AT SEA 2.5 25.5 9.5 14.5 14 33 9.5 4 13.5 7-tone scale Range #VII-8	I-II	A B C D = E B C D´

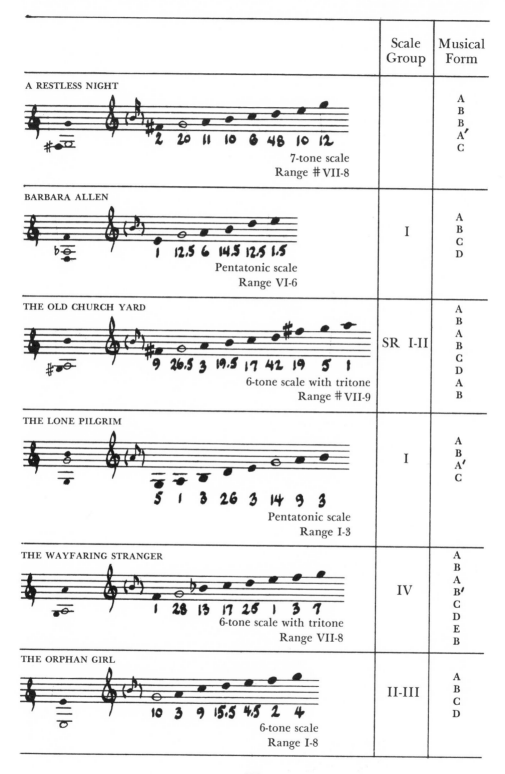

	Scale Group	Musical Form
A RESTLESS NIGHT — 7-tone scale, Range #VII-8		A B B A' C
BARBARA ALLEN — Pentatonic scale, Range VI-6	I	A B C D
THE OLD CHURCH YARD — 6-tone scale with tritone, Range #VII-9	SR I-II	A B A B C D A B
THE LONE PILGRIM — Pentatonic scale, Range I-3	I	A B A' C
THE WAYFARING STRANGER — 6-tone scale with tritone, Range VII-8	IV	A B A B' C D E B
THE ORPHAN GIRL — 6-tone scale, Range I-8	II-III	A B C D

	Scale Group	Musical Form
MANDY Pentatonic scale Range V-5	I	A A' B C
ALLEN BAIN 7-tone scale Range # VII-6	I-II	A B C D A B C E
DON'T GO OUT TONIGHT, MY DARLING 6-tone scale Range V-6	I-II	A B A C
LITTLE JIM 7-tone scale Range V-5	I-II	A B A' C D E A'' F
NO TELEPHONE IN HEAVEN 6-tone scale Range V-6	I-II	A B A C
HANGMAN ON THE GALLOWS TREE 7-tone scale Range V-7	II-III-IV	A B = A' C D E

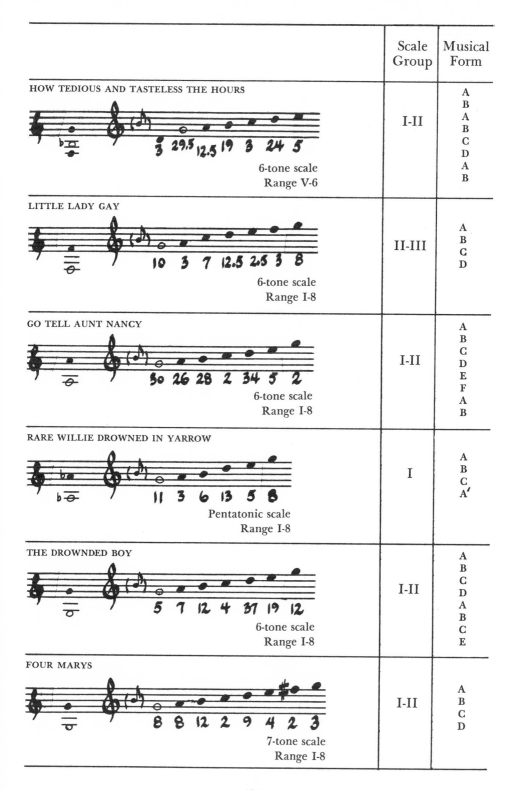

	Scale Group	Musical Form
HOW TEDIOUS AND TASTELESS THE HOURS 6-tone scale Range V-6	I-II	A B A B C D A B
LITTLE LADY GAY 6-tone scale Range I-8	II-III	A B C D
GO TELL AUNT NANCY 6-tone scale Range I-8	I-II	A B C D E F A B
RARE WILLIE DROWNED IN YARROW Pentatonic scale Range I-8	I	A B C A'
THE DROWNDED BOY 6-tone scale Range I-8	I-II	A B C D A B C E
FOUR MARYS 7-tone scale Range I-8	I-II	A B C D

171

	Scale Group	Musical Form
LADY MARGARET AND LORD WILLIAM 6-tone scale Range VII-8	II-III	A B C D E
THE GOLDEN WILLOW TREE Pentatonic scale Range I-8	II	A B C D

Notes to the Songs

No attempt will be made here to give full annotation to each of the songs. Rather, where possible, references will be made to those bibliographical sources which bring together data and provide similar texts which will allow for a further exploration into the backgrounds of the song by those interested. My arrangement of the songs follows that of the book. The sources to which I refer are:

Barry, Phillips. *The Maine Woods Songster.* Cambridge: Harvard University Press, 1939.

Belden, Henry Marvin. *Ballads and Songs Collected by the Missouri Folk-Lore Society.* University of Missouri Studies, Vol. XV, No. 1. Columbia, Mo., 1940; 2nd ed., 1955.

Brown, Frank C. *The Frank C. Brown Collection of North Carolina Folklore.* 7 vols. Durham: Duke University Press, 1952-61. See especially Vol. II, *Folk Ballads from North Carolina,* ed. Henry M. Belden and Arthur Palmer Hudson, 1952; and Vol. III, *Folk Songs from North Carolina,* ed. Henry M. Belden and Arthur Palmer Hudson, 1952.

Child, Francis James. *The English and Scottish Popular Ballads.* Boston: Houghton, Mifflin Company, 1882-98.

Coffin, Tristram P. *The British Traditional Ballad in North America.* Philadelphia: American Folklore Society, 1950-63.

Combs, Josiah H. *Folk-Songs of the Southern United States,* edited by D. K. Wilgus. Austin: University of Texas Press, 1967.

Davis, Arthur Kyle, Jr. *Folk-Songs of Virginia: A Descriptive Index and Classification.* Durham: Duke University Press, 1949.

Eddy, Mary O. *Ballads and Songs of Ohio.* New York: J. J. Augustin, 1939.

Gardner, Emelyn Elizabeth and Geraldine J. Chickering. *Ballads and Songs of Southern Michigan.* Ann Arbor: University of Michigan Press, 1939.

Greenway, John. *American Folksongs of Social Protest.* Philadelphia: University of Pennsylvania Press, 1953.

Henry, Mellinger Edward. *Folk-Songs from the Southern Highlands.* New York: J. J. Augustin, 1938.

Jackson, George Pullen. *Another Sheaf of White Spirituals.* Gainesville: University of Florida Press, 1952.

————. *Down-East Spirituals and Others.* New York: J. J. Augustin, 1943.

————. *Spiritual Folk-Songs of Early America.* New York: J. J. Augustin, 1937.

————. *White and Negro Spirituals.* New York: J. J. Augustin, 1943.

————. *White Spirituals in the Southern Uplands.* Chapel Hill: University of North Carolina Press, 1933.

Laws, G. Malcolm, Jr. *American Balladry from British Broadsides: A Guide for Students and Collectors of Traditional Song.* Publications of the American Folklore Society, Bibliographical and Special Series, Vol. VIII. Philadelphia, 1957.

————. *Native American Balladry: A Descriptive Study and a Bibliographical Syllabus.* Publications of the American Folklore Society, Bibliographical Series. Vol. I. Rev. ed. Philadelphia, 1964.

Lomax, John A. and Alan Lomax. *Negro Folk Songs as Sung by Lead Belly.* New York: Macmillan Company, 1936.

Pound, Louise. *American Ballads and Songs.* New York: Charles Scribner's Sons, 1922.

————. *Folk-Songs of Nebraska and the Central West, A Syllabus.* Nebraska Academy of Sciences Publications. Vol. IX, No. 3. Lincoln, 1915.

Randolph, Vance. *Ozark Folk Songs.* 4 Vols. Columbia, Mo.: State Historical Society of Missouri, 1947-50.

Sharp, C. J. *English Folk Songs from the Southern Appalachians,* edited by M. Karpeles. 2 vols. London: Oxford University Press, 1932-52.

Shay, Frank. *More Pious Friends and Drunken Companions.* New York: Doubleday, Page and Company, 1928.

Spaeth, Sigmund. *Read 'Em and Weep: The Songs You Forgot to Remember.* New York: Doubleday, Page and Company, 1927.

————. *Weep Some More, My Lady.* New York: Doubleday Page and Company, 1927.

1. "The House Carpenter's Wife"—Child 243, "James Harris or The Daemon Lover." This is an unusual variant in its use of the repeated last line with the wording changing slightly in most stanzas. Coffin, 137-39, Type C.

2. "Jesse James." Laws El. Unique final chorus.

3. "The Texas Rangers." Laws A8.

4. "My Old Cottage Home." No previous reporting.

5. "The Boys in Blue." Randolph IV 147 notes that the song was recorded by Grayson and Whitter (Victor 21139). He prints three versions.

6. "The Storm at Heber Springs." Taken from a ballet sheet in the hands of J. L. James.

7. "The Nightingale Song." Laws P14.

8. "Black Jack Davey"—Child 200, "The Gypsy Laddie." Coffin 119-22

Type A. As in "The House Carpenter's Wife," the last line is repeated but with variations. This is a more common technique with this ballad.

9. "Brisk Young Farmer"—Laws N30, "William Hall." One of many songs in Granny's repertoire on this theme.

10. "The Dying Ranger"—Laws A14.

11. "Man of Constant Sorrow." This strange song seems to have been widely sung yet seldom collected. Sharp II 233 reports a version of "I Was Born in East Virginia" with this first stanza; Davis 93 reports two versions from the Virginia archives, and a further version has been collected from the late Mrs. Marybird McAllister, Brown's Cove, Albemarle County, Virginia. The song was rewritten by Mrs. Sarah Ogan of Harlan County, Kentucky, and printed in John Greenway's *American Folksongs of Protest*, 168. Mr. Greenway collected a version of the ballad from Mrs. Ogan's sister, "Aunt Molly" Jackson. A song having the same first stanza was recorded by Emry Arthur (Paramount 3289) and the same song was often recorded by the Stanley Brothers.

12. "Rome County." For a history of this song and the story behind it, see P. B. Kirkeminde, "The Confession of Willis Mayberry," *Tennessee Folklore Society Bulletin*, XXX (1960), 7-21. It more commonly known as "The Hills of Rowan County."

13. "Brother Green"—Randolph notes that "several old-timers insist that the song was written by a Federal officer named Sutton, wounded at the battle of Wilson's Creek, near Springfield, Missouri." He prints two versions and gives many other references. Belden says the song "is said to have been composed by Rev. J. L. Simpson, late chaplain in the army . . . on the death of a brother who was killed at Fort Donaldson, February, 1867." The Brown Collection III 470-72 prints one text and lists two others.

14. "Ten Thousand Miles Away." Randolph IV, 151-52 has a pair of texts and a tune. He notes, "Several persons have told me that the authorship was claimed by an itinerant singing-teacher named Hubbard, who sold a book of his own songs in the Joplin, Missouri, mining district about 1895."

15. "La La La Chick a La Le-O." This is a version of the nursery song, "Bobby Shaftoe." It is reported as an American folksong only from Virginia (Davis 200) and North Carolina (Brown Collection III 183). For England, see Dean-Smith, 53. For a history of the song in children's books, see Iona and Peter Opie, *The Oxford Dictionary of Nursery Rhymes* (New York: Oxford University Press, 1951), 90-91.

16. "Froggie Went A-Courting." This is the most common, and perhaps the oldest of English children's ballads. It has been chronicled often, notably by G. L. Kittredge in *Journal of American Folklore*, XXXV (1922), 394-99, and Payne, *Publications of the Texas Folklore Society*, V. (1926) 5-49. The headnote in the Brown Collection III 154 gives a full list of sources. This text fits into Payne's category C.

17. "China Doll." Randolph III 46 has a version very close to this.

18. "Nishi." Just why this spiritual, "We Have Fathers Over Yonder" should be collected in a number of places as an Indian song defies explanation unless it was used by missionaries. The Brown Collection III 685 reports it a

"Cherokee Hymn" with similar gibberish lyrics. The headnote there gives printed sources and other reportings from tradition. George Foss, Jr., has collected a similar text from Kentucky.

19. "Blind Child's Prayer." Randolph IV 191-95 has three versions. The headnote lists other traditional reportings, but notes that authorship has not been determined, though the song is of the sort to which an attribution can be made.

20. "Little Lonie"—Laws F4, "Poor Omie" (John Lewis.) Brown II 690 has a description of the history of the deeds described in song.

21. "Kitty Wells." Written by Thomas Sloan in the 1860's, this song has been widely reported from traditional repertoires. The headnote in the Brown Collection III 492 gives some thirteen references and lists thirteen versions in the Brown Collection archives, of which it prints only one because of the lack of significant variations.

22. "The War Song"—Child 210, "Bonnie James Campbell," Coffin 126 notes six different reportings of this Scottish lament, often erroneously listed as a ballad. In such songs, it was understood that the audience knew the story of the hero's death, so that it is doubtful that there ever was much detail actually in the lament. However, a number of poignant touches have been lost, such as Campbell's bride and mother coming out to meet his horse but not finding him on it. Nevertheless, this the central stanza has retained its attraction. See Arthur Kyle Davis, Jr., *More Traditional Ballads of Virginia* (Chapel Hill: University of North Carolina Press, 1960).

23. "The Broke-Down Brakeman." This is not in Randolph. I have not been able to find any previous reporting of this song from tradition.

24. "The Oxford Girl." Laws P35. Laws, in his introduction to *American Balladry* 104-22 has an extensive discussion of the complicated history of this ballad so often collected and rewritten in America.

25. "Love I sit"—A "neck riddle," one of the most common in English. It is commonly known as the "Ilo Riddle" by folklorists because of a German enigmatic text. For a discussion of this and other neck riddles, see F. J. Norton, "Prisoner Who Saved his Neck With a Riddle," *Folk-Lore,* LIII (1942) 27-57.
Milk riddle—449-51 in Taylor, *English Riddles from Oral Tradition*—(Berkeley and Los Angeles, 1950).
Glove riddle—24, Taylor, *ibid.*

26. "Custer's Last Fierce Charge"—Laws A17, "The Last Fierce Charge."

27. "A Soldier of the Legion"—"Bingen on the Rhine," by Caroline E. Norton, Lady Maxwell, English poet, 1808-77. It has been much anthologized.

28. "Long Lost Love." Composed by Granny.

29. "Tom Sherman's Barroom"—Laws B1, "The Cowboy's Lament." For a study of this and the many other offspring of "The Unfortunate Rake," see Folkways Record FS3805, ed. Kenneth S. Goldstein. See also the discussion of the song in *Songs of the Cowboys*, by N. Howard "Jack" Thorpe, variants, commentary, notes, and lexicon by Austin E. and Alta S. Fife (New York, 1966), 148-90. This version is closer to the broadside "sailor" texts than the better-known "Streets of Laredo."

30. "When the Work's All Done This Fall." Laws B3.

31. "Al Bowen." Unreported until now. "The Wreck of Number Nine" (Laws G26), mentioned as the companion piece, was written by Carson J. Robison.

32. "Merrimac at Sea"—Child 289, "The Mermaid." Coffin 157-58. The assignment of the name *Merrimac* to this ballad is unique, though other ships have been given such an honor. Here the mermaid sighting has been lost, thus bringing this text closest to Coffin's type C.

33. "A Restless Night." This previously unreported song is probably a parody of the "Comical Ditty" printed and discussed in Belden 430. This is a song of revenge against the popular "State of Arkansas" (Belden 424; Randolph III 25), and other such *blasons populaires*.

34. "Barbara Allen"—Child 84, "Bonny Barbara Allen." Coffin 82-85. This is one of the three or four most commonly reported ballads in the United States, a popularity due in part to its inclusion in popular songsters, most notably the "Forget-Me-Not Songster." Ed Cray has surveyed the various printings of the song: "'Barbara Allen': Cheap Print and Reprint" in *Folklore International* (Hatboro, Pennsylvania, 1967), 41-50.

35. "The Old Churchyard." Printed by George Pullen Jackson in two of his books, *Down-East Spirituals and Others* and *White and Negro Spirituals;* he gives sample references from shape-note hymnals. Another reporting, similar in tradition to this, is given in L. L. McDowell, *Songs of the Old Camp Ground* (Ann Arbor, Michigan, 1937), 10-11, in which the author notes: "My father, born in 1838, learned this old song in his youth, and sung it to me in my childhood; about 1890 to 1900. I have never seen it reproduced except in a little collection of old hymns that did not contain the music." Randolph IV also prints a version with a note that "several oldtime religionists in the Ozarks have told me that it was a 'Millerite' hymn."

36. "The Lone Pilgrim." The history of this song is given in notes in Randolph IV 56; Jackson, *Spiritual Folk-Songs of Early America,* 47-48; Brown III 599; Jackson, *Another Sheaf of White Spirituals,* 11. None of the histories agree, but that given by D. K. Wilgus in his article "'The White Pilgrim' Song, Legend and Fact," *Southern Folklore Quarterly,* XIV (1950) 177-84, is the fullest and most reliable.

37. "The Wayfaring Stranger." Jackson, of *Spiritual Folk-Songs of Early America,* 71, notes that the earliest known recording among the fasola folk was in the first edition of the *Sacred Harp,* 1844. There he gives a version from *Good Old Songs* (comp. Rev. C. H. Cayce, Thornton, Arkansas) which, coincidentally, is the book referred to by Granny in her discussion of "The Old Churchyard." The tune is common to a wide range of secular songs, among them "Drowsy Sleepers," "Old Virginny" and "Fair and Tender Ladies." It is noteworthy that this widely sung song has rarely been reported in collections.

38. "The Orphan Girl." Carl Sandburg's contention in his *American Songbag* (New York, 1922), 310, that this ultimately comes from a British broadside has not yet been proved. It has been widely reported in the United States, however; Belden 217 and Brown IV 388-92 survey these sources. Most versions seem to end with the death of the girl. Brown's text, on the other hand, has the rich man discover that the child is his darling niece.

Others expound upon her heavenly home. Granny's ironic ending is unique.

39. "Mandy." As Granny mentioned, this was a standard performance for the banjo-clown, Uncle Dave Macon, which he recorded as early as 1924 on Vocalion 14848. It has been recorded by many other country performers. John W. Work prints a version on page 244 of his *American Negro Songs*.

40. "Allen Bain." Previously unreported.

41. "Don't Go Out Tonight, My Darling." Randolph II 434 has a fuller text of this homiletic, as do the McDowells in *Memory Melodies*, 128, and Brown III 51-53 has three versions.

42. "Little Jim." Though this is a common situation for a sentimental song, I have not found this specific text previously reported. A similar, but unrelated piece by this name is given in Combs-Wilgus. The piece was originally a recitation as given here and was printed in a number of recitation books of th late nineteenth century, including *Delaney's Recitations No. 7* (New York, n.d.), 23. A song version was issued on sheet music by Oliver Ditson Company in 1867, with the information that "this pathetic little poem was recited by Mr. Couldock at the Walnut Street Theatre some years ago."

43. "No Telephone in Heaven." Another recitation-made-song, also to be found, among other places, in *Delaney's Recitations No. 3*.

44. "Hangman on the Gallows Tree"—Child 95, "The Maid Freed from the Gallows." Coffin 91-94 Type C.

45. "How Tedious and Tasteless the Hours." This is the well-known shape-note hymn, "Greenfields." Jackson in *Spiritual Folksongs*, 93-94, gives a number of references in fasola books. See also Jackson, *Down-East Spirituals and Others*, 136. Randolph IV 63, prints the song from a traditional source. As usual with such songs, there is little agreement concerning authorship.

46. "Little Lady Gay"—Child 79, "The Wife of Usher's Well. Coffin 77-79 Type A.

47. "Go Tell Aunt Nancy." This song presents as many scholarly problems as it does personal ones in Granny's life. The song, as she indicates, is closely related to the ubiquitous "Go Tell Aunt Rhody," whose distribution is surveyed in Brown III 177-78. However, here it is united to the story of "The Grey Goose" which we know from Huddie (Leadbelly) Ledbetter's rendition which came from Texas prisons and was used as a work song (see Lomax and Lomax, 108). The story there begins with a preacher killing the grey goose, and then the carcass wreaks its vengeance. Although the Lomaxes feel the song is unique to the prisons, Granny's "Aunt Nancy" text would suggest otherwise.

48. "Rare Willie Drowned in Yarrow"—Child 215. Coffin 130-31. Except for a fragment from Maine (Barry 292) and a confusing text from Ohio (Eddy, 69), this Scottish ballad has never been collected in the New World. Granny's somewhat defensive explanation of her understanding of the song arose because I indicated how rare the song is in the United States. Her text is clearly related to Child's C text.

49. "The Drownded Boy." As noted, a local ballad.

50. "Four Marys"—Child 173, "Mary Hamilton," Coffin 114-15. This text is unique in many ways. The introduction of the stillborn baby is previously

unreported on either side of the Atlantic. Further, of the American reportings only the Combs and the Davis texts tell the full story, and the latter begins in the middle; most American texts are confined to the final lyric stanzas.

51. "Lady Margaret and Lord William"—Child 74, "Fair Margaret and Sweet William." Coffin 70-72 Type B.

52. "The British Robberie" and "The Golden Willow Tree"—Child 153; "The Golden Vanity," Coffin 153-55. The first version is unusual in its repetition of the sinking, though Coffin's Types F and G are related. The second text is Type A.

Other Songs in the Repertoire

Sheets and recordings of these songs are on file at the Archives of the Center for Intercultural Studies in Folklore and Oral History, University of Texas at Austin. For convenience, the songs will be listed by Child and Laws numbers when applicable. Notes in quotations come from the ballet sheets.

BALLADS IN CHILD

2. "Cambree Shirt"—Coffin 23-24, "The Elfin Knight." Type A. 8 stanzas.
12. "Lord Randal"—Coffin 36-39. Type A. Thirteen stanzas, ends with sweetheart being willed "The tow and halter to hang from yon tree/ And let her hang there for the poisoning of me." The ballet sheet has the tune noted in the upper right-hand corner, which means Granny collected this within the last ten or fifteen years. This is borne out by her noting: "This international ballad can be found in most collections as Lord Randle, Lord Donald, Lord Lamtoun, Riller, John Willow, etc. A version similar to this is found in *The Ballad Book* by MacEdward Leach on pages 81-84. Four versions in this book."
13. "Blood of the Red Rooster," or "Blood on Shirt Sleeves"—Coffin 39-40, "Edward." Type A. Twelve stanzas; "blood of old red rooster," "guinea goodle pig," "old grey mare" "guinea gay hawk," "my own dear brother." According to Granny, "I don't remember where I first heard this one, but it was a long time ago."
53. "Lord Baitman"—Coffin 58-59, "Young Beichan." Type A, minus

the wedding motif; Turkish lady simply arrives and announces herself through the ring. Granny does not regularly sing this song as it does not appeal to her. "Too typical."

73. "The Brown Girl"—Coffin 68-69, "Lord Thomas and Fair Annet." Type B. Eleven stanzas; begins "Oh, mother, dear mother, come riddle me this." "This I don't remember where I learned. Have known it several years."

228. Peggy of Glasgow—"Glasgow Peggie"

As I came in from Glasgow town,
My highland troops all before me,
And the bonniest lass that e'er I saw
Lives there, they call her Peggy.

Oh, I would give my bonnie black horse
Also my good grey naggie,
Were I two hundred miles to the north
And none with me but Peggy.

Up then spoke her own dear father
And he was wondrous sorry:
"Well, might you steal my cow or yew
But you dare not steal my Peggy."

And up spoke her mother dear
And, oh, she spoke in sorrow:
"Since I have brought you up so well
Would you go away with a Highlander?"

He sat her on his bonnie black horse
Himself on his good grey naggie.
They ride over hills and over the dales
He's away with his bonnie Peggy.

Then up spoke her father the Earl
And, oh, but he spoke in sorrow:
"The bonniest lass in all Scotland
Is off away with a highland fellow."

Then up spoke this lowland lass,
And, oh, she spoke with sorrow:
"My mother will weep so bitterly
When she finds me gone tomorrow."

Then up spoke this highland lad
And he spoke not in sorrow:
"In my house there are feather beds
And they'll all be yours tomorrow."

"Oh, do you see yon nine score cows
And nine score sheep so shaggy?
They're all mine and will soon be thine
And I love you my Peggy."

"And do you see yon bonnie white house
Among the trees so shady?
I am the Earl of the Isle of Sky
And you shall be my Lady."

"All that's mine is thine, my love,
So why should your mother sorrow
For you will be my darling bride
When she misses you tomorrow."

"I can't remember where this came from, nor can I remember the tune. I just heard someone singing it while I was collecting in the last ten or fifteen years and made a ballet on it." This text is similar to Child A, which comes from Charles Sharpe's *Ballad Book* (Edinburg and London: William Blackwood and Sons, 1880). However, it lacks a number of stanzas and the final stanza here is unique. Of greatest importance are stanzas 6-8, where the changes made are toward a formulaic repetition. This, plus a number of other smaller alterations, would seem to argue that this text is authentically in oral tradition, and thus constitutes the first reporting of this ballad on this side of the Atlantic.

277. Nickity Nackity Now—Coffin 146-48, "The Wife Wrapt in Wether's Skin." Seven stanzas, first begins "I married me a wife in the month of June . . . I escorted her home in the light of the moon." Granny will not sing this song as she hasn't been able to get the whole thing together in her mind.

BALLADS IN LAWS

Native American:

B4. "Utah Carroll's Last Ride"—"Utah Carroll." 13½ double stanzas.

B5. "Little Joe, the Wrangler." Nine stanzas. Song written and copyrighted by cowboy singer and chronicler, N. Howard "Jack" Thorpe. See Thorpe and Fife, *Songs of the Cowboys*, 28-37. "This I also learned from my eldest son's singing it around 1930."

dD40. The Sinking of the Titanic"—"The Titanic." 3½ stanzas. "This version I learned from Mrs. Lora Garrett who was my close friend thirty years ago and still is."

dD41. Sinking of the Titanic—"The Titanic." V. Text is probably
related to that in Gardner, but is much fuller. Granny says she
learned this in 1913 or 1914, but doesn't remember where.

On the 17th day of April,
Nineteen hundred and twelve,
A ship by the name of Titanic
From Liverpool sailed with great swell.
She was headed for New York City
With a cargo of wealth untold,
But she ran into an iceberg
And sank in the water so cold.

Chorus:
While that mighty ship was sinking
In the cold dark ice sea,
The last the band was heard to play
Was "Nearer My God to Thee."

On board of this mighty vessel
Men of great fortune did ride,
The doctor the lawyer the merchant
The rich and the poor and their brides.
Oh, the gambler with all of his money
And the sailor went down the same,
The skipper insnared by his own cunning
The slayer now dies with the slain.

Chorus:

On the night of this awful disaster
They reveled in room and in hall
Some gambling, some dancing, some laughing
And their doom was then written on the wall.
But they drank and they laughed and they gambled
In revelry and fun galore
With never a thought of their danger
'Til the ice ripped open the floor.

Chorus:

Some on board this great vessel was rescued,
Others were left to their fate,
But 'twill all be made right at the judgment
There the crooked will all be made straight,
For a Savior who knew all about it
Rules on the land and the sea.
He knew what to them would sure happen
He knew what their ending would be.

E3. Cole Younger—Seven double stanzas. Begins "I am a man, a highway man, Cole Younger is my name." "This one I don't remember where I first heard. Has been here in the hills as long as I remember."

E16. Twenty-One Years. Three stanzas and chorus "Down on the levy, the levy so low." "This I learned around 1935 from my sons' and daughter's singing." They probably learned it from a recording.

F1. The Jealous Lover—Eight stanzas. Begins "The moon shone bright one evening."

F1. Another version—"The Philadelphia Lawyer"

>Away in a lone green valley
>Where the flowers bloom and fade,
>A Philadelphia lawyer fell in love
>With a beautiful maid.
>
>One night the stars shone brightly,
>The moon was shining too.
>Up to this maiden's cottage
>The handsome lawyer drew.
>
>Said he, "Let's take a ramble
>Down where the waters play,
>And where there's no disturbance
>We'll name our wedding day."
>
>They roamed the woods together
>This man and maiden fair.
>At last she said, "I'm weary
>Let us retrace our way."
>
>"Retrace your way, no never,"
>The young man he replied.
>"All in my arms I have you
>And here you now must die."
>
>"Oh, mercy," now she pleaded.
>"Will you not spare my life?
>For I have always loved you
>And want to be your wife."
>
>"Be my wife, no never,"
>Nor can I let you go."
>So he plunged a fatal dagger
>In her breast as white as snow
>
>The birds sing in the morning
>And lonely was the sound,
>And they found the lovely maiden
>Lying dead upon the ground.

She died not broken hearted
Nor by a lingering pain,
But from a fatal knife wound
From the man she loved in vain

The lawyer lies in prison
For the remainder of his life
For in an angry moment
He killed his promised wife.

"I first heard this version from a Mrs. McHaffey in about 1930. Mrs. McHaffey was a native of Missouri." This version should be assigned a new Laws designation, F1C. On internal evidence, it would seem that Woody Guthrie knew this version and used it as a basis for his composition called "The Great Philadelphia Lawyer."

F2. "Pearl Bryan." Five stanzas and chorus.

F14. "Henry Glenn" —"Henry Green." 9½ double stanzas.

F16. "Warren and Fuller"—"Fuller and Warren." Thirteen stanzas.

G17. "Young Charlotte." Ten double stanzas. "This I have known since I was a child."

G19. "Sinful Flirt"—"Willie Down by the Pond." Eight stanzas.

H4. "The Gambling Man"—"The Roving Gambler." Ten stanzas. The story element here is more pronounced than in most versions. The last two stanzas are unique:

I had a loving mother, she gave me good advice.
Said, "Quit your rambling gambling ways and make this girl your wife,
Make this girl your wife, make this girl your wife.
Quit your rambling gambling ways and marry a loving wife."

So I settle down in Tennessee and do what good I can.
I'll make her ever bless the day she loved this gambling man.
She loved this gambling man, she loved this gambling man.
I'll make her ever bless the day she wed this gambling man.

"I learned this song from the singing of my husband, H. P. Riddle, and Neil Starks in 1919, but have sung it very little myself—just not my type of song, I guess. My way, I consider it a man or male type."

H7. "There Was a Little Family Lived Up in Bethany"—"The Little Family." Eight stanzas. "This I learned from my mother's singing."

H23. "The Burglar Man"—"The Old Maid and the Burglar." Seven stanzas.

Broadsides:

M13. "My Rainbow 'Mid the Willows"—"Locks and Bolts." Seven

stanzas. Final stanza and the unsuccessful conclusion of courtship is unusual:

> They taken away my own true love
> And tears now wet my pillow.
> Oh, she's the only one I love
> My rainbow 'mid the willow.

N42. "A Pretty Maid in a Garden"—"Pretty Fair Maid." Eight stanzas, ends in marriage. "This song I learned from a little twelve-year-old girl (in 1920) who used to babysit for me and spent much time in my home with me. Her name was Ruby Flowers."

O38. "Fannie Moore." Nine stanzas. "This I learned from Mrs. Lora Garrett's singing. She has known it since she was a child."

P24. "Butcher Boy." 9½ stanzas. "Learned this from a schoolmate around 1912."

Q9. "Will the Weaver." Unusual ending, "Hush, Will the Weaver's Dead."

DYING SONGS

Family:

"I Hear the Low Winds Sweeping" (I Have No Mother Now). Five stanzas. Davis 117 lists a song which begins the same way. "This I learned from my mother when I was a small child."

"Put My Little Shoes Away." Six stanzas. See Randolph IV 168. "This I learned from my mother."

"The Dying Girl's Message." Sixteen stanzas. See Belden 217; Randolph IV 168-70.

"The Orphans"—"Two Little Children." Four double stanzas. See Brown II, 394-95. "Has been so long since I learned this. Remember a playmate's mother (Stella Ghent, the mother) singing to we girls when I used to spend the night there when I was only six or seven years old."

"Letter Edged in Black." Three double stanzas and a chorus. See Randolph IV 162-63.

"The Baggage Coach Ahead." Eight stanzas. See Randolph IV 163-65.

"Lonesome Dove"—"Newberry." Eight stanzas. See Brown III 359-60; and Jackson, *Spiritual Folk-Songs of Early America,* 63-65.

"Jim Blake." Eight double stanzas. "This I learned when I was ten years old." See Spaethe, *Weep Some More, My Lady;* and Shay, under the title, "The Midnight Express."

"Cruel Father." Nine stanzas. "This I first heard when I was twenty

years old in 1918; have it here on my sister Verdie's school tablet."
Story: Father kills daughter to prevent marriage, then rues the
deed.
See also "Fatal Wedding Night"; "Once I Had a Sweetheart."

Travelers:

"The Way-Worn Traveler"—"Palms of Victory." 4½ stanzas plus
chorus. See Randolph IV 64. Not related to the song in Jackson,
Down-East Spirituals and Others, 277.
"The Dying Nun." Six double stanzas. See Belden 218; Randolph IV
166-68. "This I learned as a child. Don't remember from whom."
"A Dying Soldier, or, Weary and Worn." 6½ double stanzas. "This I
learned from Leo Flippo, a timber cutter, or Charlie Morrison, who
boarded with us the winter of 1911."

SENTIMENTAL VIGNETTES OF LIFE
(other than lovers' partings)

"Pictures from Life's Other Side." Four stanzas and a chorus. See Randolph IV 31.
"Just Tell Them That You Saw Me." Four stanzas and a chorus. Paul
Dresser song from the 1890's. See Spaeth, *Read 'Em and Weep,*
220-21.
"Lover's Plea"—"Prisoner at the Bar." Six double stanzas. See Ran-
dolph IV 348. "This I had given me by a schoolmate in 1909."
"Gambling on the Sabbath Day." Eight double stanzas. See Randolph II 40.
"Mother, the Queen of My Heart." Eight stanzas. See Randolph IV
376-77.
"No One's Darling"—"I'm Nobody's Darling on Earth." Two double
stanzas and a chorus. See Randolph IV 188-91.
"Fatal Wedding Night." Seven double stanzas. See Randolph IV
277-79.
Drunkard's Lone Child. Three double stanzas and a chorus. See Randolph II 309-10; Brown III 50.
"God Never Gives Us Back Our Youth"—"The Last Farewell." Four
double stanzas. See Randolph IV 266-68. "I learned this from my
father when I was quite young—around 1908."
"My Mother Was a Lady"—"The Two Drummers." Two double
stanzas and a chorus. See Pound, *American Ballads and Songs,*
218-20, for this song by Edward B. Marks.

"Please, Mr. Bartender, Has Papa Been Here?" Seven stanzas and a chorus.

"Pictures in a Wine Glass." Ten double stanzas.

Parted Lovers:

"I'll Hang My Harp in the Willow Tree." Seven stanzas. Listed by Pound in her Syllabus, p. 14. This is not related to "Tavern in the Town" nor the song in which its chorus was based. Davis 330 lists a song which may be this one. "This is a song I heard my father and my mother sing. Have heard no one else sing it. And since 1933 have been looking in old collections, asking singers and other collectors about it."

"The Old Elm Tree." 4½ double stanzas. See Randolph IV 170-71. Barry credits the song to Sarah S. Bolton (words) and J. P. Webster (music), the latter the composer of "Sweet By and By." Pound, in her Syllabus, credits it to F. N. Crouch.

"Sea Shell Song"—"The Shells in the Ocean." Eleven stanzas. See Randolph I 341. Many versions of this song repeat one or another couplet in a kind of chorus, but the one here is unique:

> The shells in the ocean will be their deathbed.
> The waves of the ocean flow over their head.

"I learned this version from my brother-in-law in 1922, who learned it from his mother."

"Broken Engagement." Five double stanzas. See Randolph IV 283-84. "This I learned from my daughter singing and playing guitar in 1932."

"Bury Me 'Neath the Willow." Four stanzas and chorus. Randolph IV 228-30. "This I heard my father sing from my earliest remembrance."

"Dear Companion"—"Fond Affection"—"Go and Leave Me." Two versions; one 6 stanzas, one 4 stanzas and chorus. "This we girls sang during our high school days. I learned it about the year of 1916." The second is a ballet in someone else's hand.

"The Gypsy's Warning." Eight stanzas. See Randolph IV 219-22. "I first heard this sung by an elderly lady whom we all called Aunt Fanny, a Mrs. Barber. This is the version she sang as early as 1910 but am not sure of the tune, but I think I have it as nearly right as can be gotten."

"Little Black Moustache." Six stanzas. See Randolph III 128-30; Brown II 479-80.

"Red River Valley." Nine stanzas and a chorus. See Randolph IV 202-204; Brown III 305-306.

"It Would Have Been Better For Us Both." Three stanzas and a chorus. See Randolph IV 533-34.

"Once I Had a Sweetheart." Ten stanzas. See Randolph IV 310-13; Brown II 374-75.

"Barney McCoy." Three stanzas and a chorus. See Randolph IV 291-92.

"Charley Brooks." Six double stanzas. See Randolph IV 210, 212. "This I learned as a small child."

"Little Darling." Three stanzas. Randolph IV 208-209, has two versions which he lists with "Greenback Dollar," but this seems to be an error. "This I learned from Lora Garrett."

"Listen to the Mocking Bird." Two stanzas and a chorus. See Pound, *Syllabus*, 37. "I learned this when I was ten, in 1911, from Edith Blackburn."

"After the Ball." 2½ double stanzas and a chorus. See Pound, *Syllabus*, 52. "This I learned from Charlie Morrison in 19 and 10."

"Give My Love to Nell"—"Jack and Joe." Three double stanzas plus a chorus. Randolph IV 336. "This I learned from my father when I was a child."

Religious Songs:

"The Model Church." Six double stanzas. Pound, 51 and Davis, 301, both list this in their archival syllabi.

"My Mother's Bible."—Three stanzas and a chorus. "Taught me by my mother when I was a child. Do not know if it was ever published."

"He Is Just the Same Today." Three stanzas and a chorus. "This I learned from my father."

Granny's repertoire also includes at least one hundred songs from the shape-note hymnal repertoire.

Comic Songs:

"Sod Shanty on the Claim." Two stanzas and a chorus (text incomplete). See Pound, *Syllabus*, 24.

"When I Was Single." Seven stanzas. See Randolph III 66-69; Brown III 32-40. "This version we children used to sing on the road to and from school."

"I Want to Marry"—"I Love Little Willie."—Six two-part stanzas. See Randolph III 98-100; Brown III 361-63. "This I learned from Oren Beasly of Heber Springs, Arkansas."

Contents of Ballet Book

1. Jealous Lover
2. Two Lovers
3. Pictures from Life's Other Side
4. Gambling on the Sabbath Day
5. Cambree Shirt
6. The House Carpenter's Wife
7. The Dying Nun
8. The Dying Ranger
9. The Texas Rangers
10. Charlie Brooks
11. Jesse James
12. Little Black Moustache
13. Red River Valley
14. Letter Edged in Black
15. When the Work's All Done This Fall
16. Mother the Queen of my Heart
17. It Would Have Been Better For Us Both
18. No One's Darling
19. Sinful Flirt
20. Henry Glenn
21. My Rainbow 'Mid the Willows
22. The Old Elm Tree
23. Fatal Wedding Night
24. Drunkard's Lone Child
25. Custer's Last Fierce Charge
26. Pearl Bryan

27. Jim Black
28. Little Jim
29. Broken Engagement
30. God Never Gives Us Back Our Youth
31. Memories of a Lost Love
32. Just Tell Them That You Saw Me
33. The Dying Girl's Message
34. Al Bowen
35. Utah Carroll's Last Ride
36. After the Ball
37. A Pretty Maiden in a Garden
38. The Baggage Coach Ahead
39. Once I Had a Sweetheart
40. My Mother Was a Lady
41. The Burglar Man
42. Sod Shanty on the Claim
43. Barney McCoy
44. Two Little Children
45. Pictures in a Wine Glass
46. Allen Bain
47. Lonesome Dove
48. Sinking of the Titanic
49. Little Lady Gay
50. The Golden Willow Tree
51. Warren and Fuller
52. Please, Mr. Bartender, Has Papa Been Here?
53. The Butcher Boy
54. Kitty Wells